Asian and Jungian
Views of Ethics

Recent Titles in
Contributions in Philosophy

Asian and Jungian Views of Ethics

EDITED BY
Carl B. Becker

Under the auspices of
The Uehiro Foundation on
Ethics and Education

Contributions in Philosophy, Number 66

GREENWOOD PRESS
Westport, Connecticut • London

Library of Congress Cataloging-in-Publication Data

Asian and Jungian views of ethics / edited by Carl B. Becker.
     p. cm.—(Contributions in philosophy, ISSN 0084–926X ; no. 66)
    "Under the auspices of the Uehiro Foundation on Ethics and Education."
    Includes bibliographical references and index.
    ISBN 0–313–30452–1 (alk. paper)
    1. Ethics, Oriental. 2. Jungian psychology. I. Becker, Carl B., 1951– . II. Series.
BJ962.A85 1999
170—dc21   98–20069

British Library Cataloguing in Publication Data is available.

Library of Congress Catalog Card Number: 98–20069
ISBN: 0–313–30452–1
ISSN: 0084–926X

First published in 1999

Greenwood Press, 88 Post Road West, Westport, CT 06881
An imprint of Greenwood Publishing Group, Inc.

Printed in the United States of America

The paper used in this book complies with the Permanent Paper Standard issued by the National Information Standards Organization (Z39.48–1984).

10 9 8 7 6 5 4 3 2 1

Contents

Preface

Allow me a few words about the background of our Foundation. My father, Tetsuhiko Uehiro, was in Hiroshima when the first atomic bomb was
dropped on human beings on August 6, 1945. For months he suffered from
the effects of the radiation, but came to realize that he was being kept alive
by a greater force than his own will—a divine force of nature which required him to work for the good of all humankind. Overlooking devastated
Hiroshima, he declared that "World peace depends on each individual's
elimination of the mental causes of conflicts." He devoted the remainder
of his life to teaching the removal of hate and conflict through humility,
introspection, and hard work. His teachings included rising early in the
morning, cleaning public and private places for the public good, opening
one's heart in front of others, and listening to others uncritically. Over the
decades, his movement, the Practical Ethics Association, came to number
over 4 million members.

The Association is grounded upon several simple but important ethical
truths. Our view of nature, taken from traditional Japanese philosophies,
is that man is but a small part of nature, not over and against nature, as
David R. Loy has argued. It sees the unhappinesses of life as corrective
warning signs coming from nature itself, even as Robert Aziz's discussion
of Jungian synchronicity would hold. Psychologically speaking, there are
no accidents; everything has meaning, and what we see in others often
reflects what we are in ourselves, as Robert Bosnak has pointed out. We
must transform our psyches before we can produce moral action, and this
psychic transformation entails relinquishing attachment to rank, money,
and status, as Carl B. Becker has argued. The Association believes in the
importance of moral *form*, after which the mind naturally follows. Rituals,

while capable of being overdone, in fact embody and symbolize important moral relationships, especially between family members. Finally, the Association places great importance on the teaching of ethical behavior within the family. (It should be mentioned in passing that none of these authors was instructed about what to write; they express only their own views, and not the views of the Foundation.)

I have inherited the legacy of this Practical Ethics Association, and established the Uehiro Ethics Foundation. The Foundation was established in 1987, not as an agent of the Practical Ethics Association, but as a neutral, research-supporting foundation and information center for the advancement of the teaching of ethics in Japan, with an eye to discovering international if not universal normative ethics which can be taught in educational settings. The Foundation is entirely non-partisan, and supports research regardless of the age, sex, race, or religious creeds of its researchers. The Foundation, like the Association, attempts to spread the understanding and practice of morality in Japan and around the world. However, unlike the Association, which consists of members and "followers" of the teachings, the Foundation supports research in ethical theory and education by leading scholars in universities and academic institutions at home and abroad. Our Foundation has supported international conferences on ethical subjects in Europe, America, and Japan, in cooperation with the Carnegie Council and the Eranos Foundation, and with the support of other Japanese public and private institutions.

While the Foundation is concerned to work toward universal and normative ethics, it is equally concerned that these ethics not be unduly dominated by the traditional strictures of Western religions alone. Consequently, we are particularly concerned to find ethical approaches which involve non-Western and/or non-traditional approaches to ethics. At this time, our Foundation has called together five eminent scholars of ethics to write about their non-traditional approaches to ethics; this book is the culmination of their work to date, for which we thank them all. I would also like to express a word of thanks to all those who have supported the work of our Foundation financially as well as spiritually, and those who have worked so hard to produce this book in English.

Eiji Uehiro, Spring 1998

Asian and Jungian Views of Ethics

1

Introduction and Overview

The time has come to rethink ethics. Ethics can no longer be handed down as a simple set of monolithic, unicultural rules like the Ten Commandments or the Confucian Classics. This is not to say that the Ten Commandments or the Confucian Classics were wrong. On the contrary, they were indispensable to the stability of their respective civilizations and contain common truths still indispensable to humankind today. Rather, the coming together of peoples from all over the globe has given rise to new interest in Asian and non-prescriptive ethical systems. This book brings together the insights of five distinguished scholars on ethical issues. Allow me to briefly introduce each author's contributions, and proffer a few insights about each, before you begin reading their scholarly texts.

Philologist Steven Karcher, of the Swiss Eranos Foundation, has long worked with the *I-Ching* and with Chinese Taoism. His chapter (Chapter 2) is both a critique of European Christianity and an argument that morality means coming into harmony with a larger universal whole. Karcher begins by acknowledging that traditional ethics consists of both moral standards and social sanctions, involving the control of the irrational psyche by the rational mind. Social norms and ideals of behavior help individuals relate to groups without conflict, and preserve the cohesiveness of the groups, even at the expense of individual freedoms or self-realization.

However, Karcher proposes a drastically different "deconstructive" view of ethics. He argues that "ethic" also means connecting to our inner selves, through which we can then achieve a psychic connection with the universe. Our inner selves have an undeniably dark "shadow" side, an "underworld of the spirit" which was suppressed in the West for centuries by organized Christianity. Karcher sees *I-Ching* divination as one method to break through the hierarchical rational thinking of the Western Christian tradition and re-connect ourselves to the primal spirits of the universe.

According to Karcher, the *I-Ching* enables a search for occult individual meaning through the interpretation of the "divine" symbols of the book. Like Greek oracles before it, the *I-Ching* offers a "map of the confluence of the user's psyche and the universe." As we study the patterns of heaven and earth, and interpret them to apply to our own experience, we achieve spiritual healing or wholeness connecting us with the rest of the universe. Whether consciously summoned or not, divine powers are present in the *I-Ching* which reveal themselves through symbols; they enable us to heal our troubled souls by bringing ourselves more into accord with the will of heaven. This harmony with the universe and healing of the soul is Karcher's aim in ethical behavior. The *I-Ching*'s divinatory symbols help to reveal these possibilities within human consciousness.

In response to the question, "What should we do in an ethical dilemma?" Karcher might respond that "we should cast, read, or consult the *I-Ching*, and follow the ethical guidance of its symbols to bring us into greater harmony of spirit." Indeed, this suggests some valuable possibilities long recognized in the East, but perhaps new to Western ethicists. However, the problem remains that not every interpretation of the *I-Ching* is equally moral. Interpretations may be more or less perverse or humane. Who is to say which interpretation is truly moral? We might believe that we discovered the morality of universal harmony, when in fact we just interpreted the *I-Ching* to justify our personal plans or preferences. How are we to know that we are not fooling ourselves? Proper spiritual sensitivity is presupposed, but its absence is precisely what causes many moral errors.

Robert Bosnak seeks a basis for ethical judgment in Chapter 3. He attempts to ground ethics on internal feelings of revulsion rather than on prescriptive social rules. He argues that the uneasiness which we instinctively experience when facing moral mistakes demonstrates their unethical nature, that we are out of harmony with our bodies and with the universe.

Bosnak recommends dream incubation and analysis to put us in touch with our ethical feelings. Dreams symbolically reveal to us our insights about our viscerally based moral feelings. According to Bosnak, we must recognize our visceral feelings fully and then connect those feelings with our moral judgments. Admission and awareness of our "dark" shadow side is a first step to making us more forgiving of the mistakes of others. It also rejects thinking of any single society as superior to any other. We gain the ethical insight that our focusing our frustrations on others is largely mistaken; in fact, most moral problems are inherent within ourselves.

Ethical instinct can be trained, Bosnak says, by increasing our sensitivity to our bodies and dreams. We can become more conscious of and act more voluntarily upon our viscerally experienced moral emotions. However, unreflective action upon impulse can be as dangerous as repression of such impulses; an analytical balance is needed. Thus, refined outrage can lead to action toward greater justice, whereas repressed outrage might lead to physical disease, and unreflected expression of outrage leads only to conflict and polarization. We must avoid ethical insensitivity to moral claims at the same time as we avoid moral oversensitivity, which leads to depressive guilt and inability to act constructively. So refined reflection is required. By training our sense of ethics, we can achieve an ethical creativity, not bound by previous rules, but leading to solutions which help everyone.

In response to the question, "What should we do in an ethical dilemma?" Bosnak would respond, "See how your body feels, and see what your dream images tell you about the rightness of the situation." This, too, is an important insight. Philosophers ever since David Hume have recognized that ethics are in some sense based on the "passions" or feelings. However, Bosnak's approach is not without its own problems. First, our visceral feelings (disgust, remorse, revulsion, etc.,) generally occur only *after* a crime, war, or moral tragedy has occurred. We suffer only after the fact, not in advance; if we suffered in advance, we might never commit moral misdeeds in the first place. Now we can try to imagine in advance all possible consequences and our feelings toward them. But it is precisely because we cannot do this adequately that we make moral mistakes. So the bodily-response approach provides a post facto rather than a preventive approach to immoral behavior.

Second, visceral reactions often fail to tell us what is wrong, as in Bosnak's own example. A client is cheating on his wife. He imagines telling her of his cheating, feels pain in doing so, and decides that the ethical thing is not to tell her that he is cheating. However, he fails to feel any pain in the act of cheating itself. Bosnak's conclusion is that his patient should not tell his wife but should continue to cheat on her. However, there are good reasons to think that the cheating in itself is what is wrong, and that the pain that both the patient and the wife feel are the result of the wrongness of the cheating, not of the wrongness of the confession. As long as the patient and the counselor fail to recognize a connection between the pain and cheating itself, they will mistakenly conclude that cheating is acceptable as long as it is undiscovered. This is like a criminal telling himself that it is acceptable to steal as long as he is not caught, because he cannot stop stealing and feels no remorse, and moreover that he should not turn himself in because he feels uneasiness in imagining himself discovered.

Finally, for the purposes of our Foundation's search for more universal ethical directions, the visceral emotion approach is inescapably subjective. It is possible that we may become more sensitive to our feelings and dreams, but what about people who do not share our feelings of revulsion? If ethics is the business of determining right and wrong, good and bad, then how are we to adjudicate a situation where some party is simply morally "color-blind" or insensitive? Can we come up with the same sorts of standards for moral blindness as we can come up with for color-blindness? Conversely, can we be sure whether an upset feeling in our stomach or a bad dream is due to a moral revulsion, to a childhood trauma, or simply to something we ate before getting on an airplane?

Robert Aziz is another Jungian who rejects rule-centered ethics for person-centered ethics. But while Bosnak bases this center in human *bodily* experience, Aziz sees it in human *synchronistic* experience, or in the tendency of humans to imbue events with meaning. For Aziz, ethics is not so much a matter of learning how to make decisions in specific situations, but rather of developing a personal character or quality of ethicalness which pervades our lives and actions.

In Chapter 4, Aziz begins by noting Europe's shift in the twentieth century from external historical religion to internal experiential religion, from God dominating nature to god expressed through Nature. In this changing context, ethics should flow from an exchange between the consciousness of external duties and the subconsciousness of internal impulses to the good. He recognizes first the problem, already noted by the previous authors, of correctly interpreting the meaning of the interchanges between the conscious and the unconscious, and second, the problem of grounding this meaning in one's own moral life and action. Like Karcher in his concern for symbols embodying meaning, and like Bosnak in his contention that these symbols are often revealed through our dreams, Aziz feels that our dreams symbolize not only our subconscious problems but also the paths to their resolutions.

Aziz holds that the dominantly inner orientation of Jungian psychiatry has *weakened* its inherently ethical dimensions, but that Jung was very conscious of external forces of nature trying to educate humans into greater consciousness of rightness and harmony. Being ethical, then, means transforming ourselves by recognizing new meanings in and perspectives on our lives, not only in our dreams and bodily feelings, but in the events that happen to us.

In Aziz's view, Nature itself is intrinsically moral; it takes external and undeniable "compensatory" action to enable us to realize our moral mistakes and lead us to self-realization. In simpler terms, moral mistakes lead us not only to bad dreams and upset feelings, as Bosnak says, but also to events which shake us up and force our re-examination of our lives. Aziz gives examples of actual calls, of letters, and of minor crises which are so timed as to be indubitably connected with inner mental events. For Aziz, as for Jung, the psychic and physical are ultimately inextricably interconnected. Egocentric refusal to give up mistaken conclusions blocks our ethical growth, wastes our time, and ultimately places us at odds not only with ourselves but with the universe of which we are a tiny but integral part. If we can come to see ourselves as co-existing with and not separate from the ethical universe, then we ourselves will become naturally more ethical, making decisions more ethically appropriate to the well-being of ourselves and of the whole.

For Aziz, the question, "What should we do in an ethical dilemma?" must be answered by consulting both the symbols of our dreams and ethical imaginations, and the meanings of the events which occur synchronistically throughout our lives. This is an almost karmic recognition that everything we do ultimately rebounds back to ourselves again; everything that appears to "happen to us" is in fact something that we have either caused or need to learn from in an ethical sense.

In Chapter 5, David R. Loy advances this insight based on his studies of Taoism and Buddhism. Loy makes the case that ethics can no longer be concerned merely with interpersonal relationships, but must face environmental relationships of people to the world. To properly approach a new environmental ethic, we must overturn prevailing Judeo-Christian capitalist views of human dominion over nature. We must view nature not as raw materials for human use, but as our life support system, indeed, as not separable from ourselves. Loy uses the three non-dualist perspectives of Taoism, Buddhism, and deep ecology to advance his argument.

Traditional ethics tend to concern themselves with issues like intentions and standards of good. Taoists critiqued traditional ethical concerns with intentions, because they tend to reduce everything to mere *means* to something else, and the intrinsic value of each process is overlooked. Taoism critiques traditional ethical standards as themselves creating a bifurcation between good and evil; the very act of defining one position or action as "good" entails the criticizing of an "opposite" position or action as "evil."

According to Taoism, such discrimination is contrary to nature. Taoism does not reject all morality nor renounce all moral action, but rather seeks a selflessness *transcending* moral codes of self-versus-other. This transcendental perspective enables us to overcome our desires to control others, to use others as means to our own satisfactions, and to dominate nature.

It is true that the Buddha laid down hundreds of guidelines for action. After he entered nirvana, these became canonized into the moral codes of the Pali scriptures called the *Vinaya*. Loy points out that for the Buddhist, true morality is not following a set of prescribed rules and regulations, but generosity without thought of return. The Buddhist loves the "other" not as an "other" deserving of love or sympathy, but realizing that ultimately the "other" is non-different from self. This is clearly exemplified in Thich Nhat-Hanh's moving description of a sheet of paper embodying the cloud and sunshine that watered the tree that made it, the food and breath of the logger who logged it, the whole ecosystem and family of humankind which are intertwined with its existence. Thus, both "self" and "other" are delusions which must be transcended, and the action which spontaneously emerges is naturally ethical when discrimination is transcended. In Loy's terms, the center of Buddhist morality is *non-contrivance*, not trying to get anything from or for anyone.

The third complementary philosophy to which Loy refers is the "deep ecology" position represented by Aldo Leopold. This philosophy maintains that right action is that which tends to maintain the integrity, stability, and beauty of the universe. Like Buddhism and Taoism, but more contemporarily, it argues that human-centered, economically based thinking must give way to land-centered thinking to preserve the balance of nature. Like Buddhism and Taoism, it defines self-realization as the realization that self is non-different from all other organisms. This leads to the position that every being and every event has an undeniable and intrinsic worth, which cannot be valued less than that of any other. Then questions of intention, of utility and economic justification simply cease to apply, and we reach the Taoist conclusion that it is best to "let things be."

Loy is not unaware of the paradox lurking here: that only humans have the reflexive ability to think of themselves as other than and different from the nature in which they live; only humans have the ability to reflect upon their actions as good and bad; only humans have the power to destroy or consciously preserve the balance in the ecosystem in which they participate. If it is this consciousness of separation which brings humans pain, then it is humans alone who must regain a consciousness of our unity with all beings. So for Loy, ethical rightness is a consciousness of non-difference and non-discrimination, a "loving the world as oneself," leading naturally to action. However, this is a lofty goal which only a minority of sages and enlightened beings realize in practice.

In Carl B. Becker's chapter (Chapter 6), a more pragmatic level of environmental ethics is addressed; he seeks practical rules for environmental preservation grounded in a consciousness of interconnectedness. Becker begins from the Buddhist basis of the limitation and suffering inherent in all material existence. He applies this insight to ethical problems, particularly those of environmental preservation, recycling, and population growth. Becker discusses modern consumption-and-waste cycles, and the possibilities of recycling from the recognition that the earth is fundamentally "sacred." (In Loy's terms, this might be rephrased to read that the earth is fundamentally of intrinsic value for itself and not for any other purpose.) Becker also notes that the costs of recycling and preservation must be built into our economic system.

All of these ethical rules involve a limitation of personal desires, or rather a cultivation of personal desires away from the self-serving and animal, toward the transpersonal and universal. Only when such desires are achieved will peace of mind be possible; conversely, without peace of mind in our own being, craving for external approbation and material goods will perpetually plague all our attempts to be ethical.

In response to "What should we do in an ethical dilemma?" Becker answers that we should seek solutions which do not depend on personal desires or capital gains, but which lead toward sustainable coexistence of humans and the ecosystem, which promote equanimity and cooperation over stress and competition.

Becker then applies this philosophy to the role of ethical education in teaching world-preserving values. He critiques previous values-clarification curricula, and gives examples of successful programs from the American context. He stresses the needs to adapt these to a more Asian/Buddhist framework and to publicize and exalt moral values through the power of the modern mass media. While this theory is far simpler than its practice, it is indeed the sort of direction which the Uehiro Ethics Foundation desires to promote.

2

Crossed Paths, Crossed Sticks, Crossed Fingers: Divination and the *Classic of Change* in the Shadow of the West

STEPHEN KARCHER

WHICH WAY I FLY IS HELL . . .

Der Störende ist Gott.

C. G. Jung[1]

Lucifer's realization in Milton's *Paradise Lost*—"*Which way I fly is Hell; myself am Hell*"[2]—could be a motto for the *Zeitgeist* of the twentieth century. Freud began his *Interpretation of Dreams* with the prefix: *Flectere si nequo superos Acheronta movebo* / "If I cannot bend the Gods on high, I will at least set Acheron in uproar"; Marx's *Das Kapital* put the underworld slums of industrial London at the center of political thought; Picasso's *Les demoiselles d'Avignon* offered a demonic brothel filled with savage masks as the locus of beauty; and Rimbaud's *Saison en enfer* proposed a hallucinatory poetic that loosed the caged voices of desire through a "systematic derangement of all the senses."[3] In search of some new vision, Western culture and the rest of the world, influenced by the West's wealth, science, and wars, has been irresistibly drawn into what Jung called the "Shadow." In 1934, Jung cited a European theologian's dream, paradigmatic of this culture at the brink:

[I] dreamed that I saw on a mountain a kind of Castle of the Grial. [I] went along a road that seemed to lead straight to the foot of the mountain and up it. But as [I] drew near [I] discovered . . . that a chasm separated [me] from the mountain, a deep darksome gorge with underworldly water rushing along the bottom. A steep path led downwards.[4]

"This water is no figure of speech," Jung observed, "but a living symbol of the dark psyche (*CW* 9i, § 33) . . . earthy and tangible, it is also the fluid of the instinct-driven body, blood and the flowing of blood, the odor of the beast, carnality heavy with passion" (*CW* 9i, § 41).*

Jung saw a drive in this breakdown. In 1928, writing on "The Spiritual Problem of Modern Man," he maintained:

Our age wants to experience the psyche for itself. It wants original experience and not assumptions. How else can we explain this zeal, this almost fanatical worship of everything unsavory? It is because these things . . . are of the substance of the psyche and therefore as precious as fragments of manuscripts salvaged from ancient middens. . . . [The] crux of the spiritual problem today is to be found in the fascination which the psyche holds for modern man . . . [it] touches those irrational and—as history shows—incalculable psychic forces which transform the life of peoples and civilizations in ways that are unforeseen and unforeseeable. (*CW* 10, § 173, 177, 191)

Writing in 1956 on "The Undiscovered Self," he further remarked:

We are living in what the Greeks called the *kairos*—the right moment—for a "metamorphosis of the Gods," of the fundamental principles and symbols. This peculiarity of our time, which is certainly not of our conscious choosing, is the expression of the unconscious man within us who is changing. (*CW* 10, § 585)

Thus, according to Jung, this "symptom and symbol of a mood of universal destruction and renewal that has set its mark on our age" has a *telos*, a goal or purpose. And it has an *ethos*, an ethic or imperative, for it is the individual who is the "makeweight who tips the scales" in the death and rebirth of the Gods (*CW* 10, § 586). If the drive of our time is to experience the underworld of the psyche, then the task imposed upon us is to achieve an awareness of this "psychic connection." For it is in psyche, in the fluid, dark, interior world where blood, thought, and image mix, that all change takes place.

The *I Ching*, the ancient Chinese Book of Oracles, enters modern culture through just this Luciferian *kairos*, this "nick" in the hierarchy of values. It constellates first "superstition" and rational condescension, and behind that, shadow, psyche, blood-soul, fate: a pagan, magical world. I follow Jung here in maintaining that the divinatory use of the *I Ching* is not exoticism, chicanery, or superstition, but a "sign that we are beginning to relate to the alien elements in ourselves" (*CW* 13, § 72). It is the purpose of this chapter to look more closely at these "alien elements." This will involve a discussion of divination and its repression in European culture;

---

*References to Jung's *Collected Works (CW)* are to Bollingen series XX, vols. 1–20, trans. R. F. C. Hull (Princeton, NJ: Princeton University Press, 1957–1979).

a look at "live" divinatory practices in a non-European context; and a consideration of how the *I Ching* as the "living spirit of the East" (*CW* 15, § 78) shaped Jung's own approach to the psyche. My concern is the ethical need to relate to these inner aliens, for divinatory images can give a voice to that "unconscious man within us who is changing."[5]

ETHOS AND DAIMON

Ethics is commonly defined[6] as the discipline of studying what is good and bad, right and wrong, in terms of moral duty or obligation. The term's meanings include: a group of moral principles or values; a theory of morality; the principles of conduct governing a profession; the ideals of character manifested by a race, nation, or people. This last is particularly accented in a cognate term, *ethos*, which refers to: character, sentiment, moral nature; the beliefs and ideals that identify a group or community; the complex of moral values underlying major patterns of behavior in a culture or society.

This double sense of ethics as moral standard and social character antedates Aristotle, who defined *ethos* as both the characteristic spirit of a people and a rationalizing of that spirit: a control of the irrational parts of the psyche by the reason or *logos (Rhetoric* II, 12–14). The rationalization of ethos into ethics involves a discipline of the passive or autonomous activations of the soul (*pathe*) in pain, fear, pleasure, desire, pity. This "making rational" of ethos as a common ideal of behavior is prior to and acts as a base for the activity of the understanding or *dianoia (Nicomachean Ethics* 1139a). It is created through the formation of habits which embody ideals of behavior (Plato, *Laws*, 792e).

The English words ethos and ethics come from the Greek *ethos*, which refers to: custom, trait, usage; the haunt, lair, or cave of an animal; manners, or disposition. A cognate, *ethas*, signifies: domestic, tamed, accustomed to something. The root of the term is thought to be the Indo-European seed-syllable *seu*.[7] It is a third person reflexive pronoun which refers back to the subject (Latin *sui*, French *se*, German *sich*) and designates the social group as a self-conscious entity: (we-our-)selves. Thus, the root of the word ethics relates the individual to the group as a reflexive action, turning or bending the subject back on social identity. In this root context, a thought or act that defines the individual in terms of a group is *ethical*; the individual is *ethical* insofar as she or he reflects that relation.

Yet there is another sense of the word, an under-sense or under-standing that reflects another, de-constructive, language. When we place a problem in this language, we re-enter a very old tradition of "day-world" and "night-world" which has "always-already" shadowed the question.[8]

The *ethos* of humans, said Heraclitus, is *daimon* (Fragment 119, Freeman).[9] This statement by the pre-Socratic philosopher called "the Riddler," "the Dark," a "Dionysian thinker," is like a dream image or an oracle's response. Its sharp contours reflect an ambiguity of significance, a multiplicity of meaning, that pulls the ground from under our feet. The *terra firma* of social relation becomes *ge, chthon, Hades*. We are in the underworld.

Other of Heraclitus' cryptic remarks fill out the context, connecting *ethos* as *daimon* with sleep, dream, psyche, cosmos. "The waking share one common world; the sleeping turn aside each man into a world of his own" (Fragment 89, Freeman). "Thinking is common to all" (Fragment 113, Freeman) but "psyche has its own logos which grows according to its needs" (Fragment 115, Freeman). "When we are alive [awake; in the common world of thought] our souls are dead and buried in us; when we die [sleep; enter Hades and the realm of images] our *psychoi* come to life again and live" (Fragment 26, Cornford). And most paradoxically: "Sleepers are the workers . . . collaborators in what goes on in the universe" (Fragment 75, Wheelwright).

Heraclitus' *ethos* turns us aside from "thought" which is normative and communal into the underworld of dream and psychic image—what the ancients called the Kingdom of Hades. It suggests a very different kind of collaboration with "what goes on in the universe." Most of all, it involves us with the *daimones*, the underworld images which are living units of the unconscious psyche"—the "architects of dreams and symptoms" (*CW* 8, § 210).

PAGANS AND CHRISTIANS: *IN HOC SIGNO VINCES*[10]

> Think not that I come to send peace on the earth; I come not to send peace but a sword.
>
> *Matthew* 10, 34

The active images or "living units" of the psyche have another conflict-ridden context. It is epitomized by the Late Latin shift in the meaning of the word *daimon* from "spirit or genius" to "evil spirit, demon, devil." This semantic shift marks the end of what has been called the Antique World,[11] a border that is psychological as well as historical. As Jung observed, although the Dionysian processions, the chthonic Mysteries, and the theriomorphic representations of the Gods have vanished, "all our lives we possess, side by side with our . . . directed and adapted thinking, a fantasy-thinking which corresponds to this antique state of mind" (*CW* 5, § 36). This "fantasy-thinking" produces "a world picture very different from that of conscious thinking," normatively called pathological, autoerotic, schizophrenic, sociopathic *(CW* 5, § 37). The violent antagonism between these two ways of knowing—the shadowing of fantasy by the normative intellect—is a part of the crisis of the present. Behind its "disenchantment of the world," this antagonism portrays a decisive shift in Western culture that split off the "Christian" from the "pagan," the spirit from the soul.

The New Testament uses the words *ethnoi* and *ta ethne*: the people of the tribes or nations for "pagan" or "heathen"—pejoratives for those who are not transcendental monotheists. In contrast, the Jews were seen as one people, because they were united by one God and one Law. In spite of the political authority of the Roman Empire, the *ethnoi* presented a multiplicity of centers, not a monolithic culture. Christians characterized them by certain practices: the use of images and "idols" in their worship; a multiplicity of gods; oracles and divination as the "speech" of these gods; and *porneia*, "fornication," root of the English word *pornography*. This last term is a particular clue to the shadow projected on pagan imagination, for it equates "non-normative" sexual practices with coming into contact with a spirit other than the Father. Finally, the *ethnoi*, pagans or *hellenes* (Greeks) are "people of this world," the *cosmos*,[12] and "people of this time," the *aion*. They are linked to the cosmos through their daimonic images; their intelligence (*nous*) and their wisdom (*sophia*) are centered on these *daimones*.[13]

The *ethnoi* lived in what one scholar has called the "rustling universe of late classical paganism," an immediate yet imaginatively very deep cosmos.[14] The late Hellenistic landscape of this "rustling universe" was at once literal and psychic. The cosmos was not experienced as a uniform expanse, but as a series of dynamic transformational spaces, *topoi* or *eikons*. These dynamic spaces were marked out by shrines, votive signs, temples, grottoes, groves, and springs that indicated sites of "close encounter" with the Gods, *daimones* and heroes[15] (Fox, 41–46). This psychic landscape, rather than a single God or Law, was the common heritage of the pagans: all classes, sexes, and ages were connected through the experience of its rites, images, and oracles.

The key word here is *epiphaneia*, the manifestation of spirit in and through the world. It marks the sacral character of this cosmos. The images and shrines of the pagan landscape did not so much commemorate the historic event of an epiphany as they re-created and re-invoked religious experience. Images and oracles marked the site of the continuing presence of the Gods; they focused the idea of the numinous, and facilitated "easy company with the Gods" in dream and vision (Fox, 675). Through these oracular images, the pagans experienced a time when the Gods moved freely among them. This "golden age" was potentially ever-present: "man and Gods in open company in a generous, burgeoning world" (Fox, 111).

The capacity for epiphany, the ability to experience spirit in the world, is the defining feature of the pagan world and of pagan "fantasy-thinking." Out of this experiential base grew Hermetic magic, the Mystery Cults, theurgy and neo-Platonic *gnosis*. The oracles, images, and verbal formulae developed in this magical tradition were seen as produced by the Gods themselves as "binding spells" through which they might be contacted. The experience is of a *daimon* or *genius*, an intermittent stream of images that regulates and shapes the personality. These epiphanic *daimones* accompany the pagans, "share their life," "hold their hand above them," near but invisible (Fox, 129, citing Maximus of Tyre). They are bound into each person's fate and act as an intermediary to the Gods and the cosmos (Plato, *Symposium*, 202d–203a; Plutarch, *De def. orac.*, 416e–418d). The pagans sensed and saw the *daimones* through the act of mutual creation that characterized their world: the magical animation, the en-souling, of an image, shrine, or temple; the incantation of an oracle or spell.

The Christian church sought to destroy just this animating connection between the world and the individual, for Christians wanted the "obedience" of pagans (*Romans* 15, 18–19). Apart from the torture of pagan prophets at major shrines, the triumphant church of the fourth century did not persecute pagans as such. Rather, it destroyed the shrines and images, cut down the groves, despoiled the landscape, and prohibited on pain of death the magical and oracular practices that gave the Gods a voice in the human world. As Eusebius recounted, Christians sent iconoclastic emissaries to "every pagan temple's recess and every gloomy cave" (Fox, 673–681).

This process, which went on throughout the fourth and fifth centuries, came to be expressed in a myth current in Europe until the Enlightenment, a myth which continues to express the psychological relations between the pagan imagination and the Christian spirit.[16] Briefly stated, the myth held that upon the advent of Christ, "the false *Oracles* and *Delusions* [were miraculously] strucken mute, and nothing to be heard at Delphos or Hammon" (Patrides, 507; quoting Sir Henry Wotton, 1654). Although the historical process was a bit different, the myth expresses a psychological truth: at the sign of the Cross the *daimones* vanish.

An ode of Milton's elaborates the effects of this advent on the cosmos. "On the Morning of Christ's Nativity," Milton tells us (stanza xix):

> The oracles are dumb,
> No voice or hideous hum
> Runs through the arched roof in words deceiving.
> Apollo from his shrine
> Can no more divine,
> With hollow shriek the steep of Delphos leaving.
> No nightly trance or breathed spell,
> Inspires the pale-eyed priest from the prophetic cell.

"A voice of weeping and great lament" is heard, rising from mountains, shores, "haunted springs," "consecrated earth," "holy hearth," altars, tombs, and groves as the nymphs, Lares, lemures, gods, and goddesses "forsake their temples dim." The "flocking shadows pale/troop to the infernal jail/each fettered ghost slips to his several grave." No other spirit, god, nymph, or daimon "longer dare abide" when "Our Babe" shows his "Godhead true."

We thus understand in a quite different way the pagan lightbringer Lucifer's[17] lament as he is cast in the role of the Adversary of an implacable God:

> Me miserable! which way shall I fly
> Infinite wrath and infinite despair?
> Which way I fly is Hell; myself am Hell
> And in the lowest deep a lower deep
> Still threatening to devour me opens wide.
>
> *Paradise Lost*, iv, 73–77

This *lumen naturae*,[18] way finder and psychopomp, is the god in our disease.

LIGHTS AND SHADOWS: LIKE(NESS) CURES LIKE

Whatever the social or philosophical dimensions[19] of the splitting-off of "Christian" from "pagan," its psychological importance cannot be overstated. The point at which the Holy Spirit demonized the pagan "spirits" was a decisive event for European culture, casting a shadow on the Gods, the flesh, and the cosmos. In its spread, European science and power demonized and repressed non-white races and traditional cultures in the same way pagan Mediterranean culture was demonized and repressed.

Phenomenologically, this splitting is a sort of continuing nuclear fission which produces two *imagos*, two *ways of relating* (CW 6, § 812) to that "unceasing stream or perhaps ocean of images and figures" which "alone constitutes immediate experience" (CW 8, § 674, 680). In the case of "conversion" to the Holy Spirit, the *psychic imago* is split off and *projected* as the shadow; it *demonizes* whatever it touches.

Shadow, as a psychological phenomenon, *occults*: it "conceals and causes to disappear from view" through a process of repression, creating a screen of moral opacity between the ego and an Other. Yet this web of hot, dark inferiority—the *porneia* and vicious behavior described in Paul's version of the pagans (for example, *Romans* 1, 24–32), *saves* as well as demonizes. Shadow carries what is most feared by the ego as a threat to its self-image. It operates through a selective amnesia, whereby "specific memories or groups of ideas are withdrawn from recollection," preserved intact outside of development with a violent negative sign (CW 17, § 199a). The general rule is: "the more negative the conscious attitude . . . the more repulsive, aggressive and frightening is the face which the dissociated content assumes" (*CW* 13, § 464). The process of "shadowing" creates a constant inner tension in the psyche between "good" and "bad," between what is and is not an ideal of "me."

Projection, in the sense of the expulsion of these negative subjective contents onto an "object" (*CW* 6, § 783), has an even more profound effect on the subject. Projection is dis-similative: it makes like things un-like. But the dissimilation soon becomes dissimulation. In projection:

a subjective content is alienated [made alien] from the subject and is . . . embodied in an object. The subject gets rid of painful, incompatible feelings by projecting them (*CM* 6, § 783). [But the effect of this projection] is to isolate the subject from the environment, since instead of a real relation to it, there is now only an illusory one. Projections change the world into the replica of one's own unknown face . . . [a] condition in which one dreams a world whose reality remains forever unattainable. (*CW* 9ii, § 17)

A sense of incompletion, sterility, and fear grows out of this situation in an ever-increasing manic spiral. In turn, this is explained as "the malevolence of the environment, and by means of this vicious circle, the isolation is intensified" (*CW* 9ii, § 17). The only way to cut into this soulless round is a confrontation with the "unknown face" of the shadow.

Jung has remarked that coming to know the shadow is the "apprentice work" (*Gesellenstück*) of the soul.[20] Shadow is psychopomp, and without shadow there is no soul—only ego. One must first become aware of shadow, a long, laborious, and unpleasant task, and to do so one must first take it seriously as an autonomous psychic being. Shadow cannot be abolished through a rational act of will; its drive for power and revenge only expresses itself more indirectly and more dangerously when cut off. Thus, one begins a long process of negotiation, a "struggle which goes on until both parties are 'out of breath.' The outcome cannot be seen in advance, only that both parties will be changed" (*CW* 14, § 514).

In a personal context, the repressive mechanisms that create shadow conceal the ego's attachments to greed, lust, cowardice, duplicitous manipulation, sadism, masochism, and the more vicious enjoyments of power. In the process of encounter, these open to reveal an enormous vitality and a great hunger for personal imaginative experience bound up with the shadowed drives. Here we find the particularly modern aspect to this age-old confrontation, the hiatus which cuts us off from the mythologizing activity of the soul.

So the concern with shadow, with the dark abyss between personal desire and the soul's images, is cultural as well as personal. However, it is approached through the most personal, painful, conflicted, shadowy, even petty problems that constellate the shadow's entanglements and desires. These "disturbers," these "aliens" who cross our paths and thwart our wills, offer a "gift to us, if we will accommodate them . . . the transformation of the world of fact into *anima* country," into soul (Giegerich, 89).

Thus, when we grapple with the shadow, we are engaged in archetypal therapy in a particular sense: therapy of an archetype.[21] By its very nature the soul has the capacity to re-join the parts split in our experience, "once it is allowed by the *individual* to return from its exile in the unconscious to its original place at the center of polarities" (Hillman, "Puer and Senex," 14, my emphasis). When we move through shadow to image, rather than through reason to fact, we are *making soul*, creating the opportunity, opening the *kairos* through which the world is re-imagined. The psyche becomes the subject, not the object, of perception, translating "reality" from dead fact to live myth. This is the "psychic connection" at the heart of the pagan cosmos, the "ritual landscape" with its points of close encounter. This is also the central concern of the act of divination itself: to move the shadow toward a psycho-active force which is manifesting itself through the symptom, demanding access to consciousness.

Similia similibus curantur, "like (likeness or likening) cures like" is a fundamental principle of traditional medicine: the cure is (like) the disease. But note that likenesses[22] are *not* sames. As in homeopathic medicine, the "cure" is the highly diluted and imaginally potentiated drug which causes the symptoms. It is the symptom transformed into a *daimon*. This transformation itself has an archetypal significance. When we touch on this dark gap between the person and the soul, "the realm of subtle bodies comes to life again . . . the physical and the psychic are once more blended" (*CW* 12, § 394).

LUMEN NATURAE AND LIMINAL SPACE

> There exists another world. But it assuredly is in this one.
>
> Paul Eluard[23]

The insight into psychic functioning developed in ancient medicine, myth, and divination is also expressed in modern archetypal psychology: "my symptoms point to my soul as my soul points to me through them. . . . Yet they are *not* of my intention; they are visitations, alienations, bringing home the personal/impersonal paradox of the soul: what is "me" is also not "mine."

This perspective on psychopathology forces us to recognize a very old psychic fact: "within the affliction is a complex, within the complex is an archetype, which in turn refers to a God. Afflictions point to Gods; Gods reach us through afflictions. . . . [they] *force themselves symptomatically into awareness*." (Hillman, *Re-visioning Psychology*, 104–5)

This is the origin of the old divinatory question: "To what god do I owe my affliction? What imagining must I perform in order to see through this opaque situation? How can I come into conscious relation with the god?"

But the heart of the divinatory practice which reveals the imaginal cosmos is not the individual God *per se*. "What the Gods notoriously want is remembrance of them, not choice among them, so that every conflict—and the very question Who?—by asking which among many, indicates them all" (Hillman, *Re-visioning Psychology*, 139).

Bouché-Leclercq, whose study of Greco-Roman divinatory systems remains a classic, expresses this difference more precisely:

The religious conceptions of Greece and Rome enclosed a profoundly mystical element implanted in all its customs . . . the belief in a permanent revelation proffered by gods to man, a sort of spontaneous intellectual aid . . . thanks to which societies and individuals could regulate their acts. The gods, from this point of view, are no longer exigent creditors or indifferent abstractions but benevolent counselors whose voice signalled, at the opportune moment, the price of the present occasion, the secrets of the past or the traps of the future. The Greeks called *mantike* and the Latins *divinatio* this *divine* light [*lumen naturae*] which added itself, like a new faculty, to human comprehension.

This divine light, the "real benefit these people drew from their religion," was:

not the product of legend and myth; on the contrary, it presided over their birth . . . an integral part of religion without being tied to any particular tradition. It was inherent in the religious sentiment itself and not to the changing forms of its manifestation . . . it grew in power as the civic forms exhausted themselves, penetrating farther each day into the individual. . . . This power, the expression of an indestructible instinct, has not yet been annulled today, and the psychologist can find its traces.[24]

Studies of "live" divinatory systems in tribal cultures[25] tell us that divination is not a random act by an aberrant individual, charlatan, or power-seeker. Divination is consistently used to yield information about questions, problems, and choices for which everyday knowledge is insufficient. It is a process deriving from a discipline and a body of knowledge. Some type of "device"—a procedure depending on chance or accident—provides the "gap" in the web of human discourse through which the spirit expresses itself by a choice among the system's signifiers. The final diagnosis and plan of action emerge from an interpretive interaction between signifier, diviner, and client.

Thus, the divinatory process is not an ideology founded on religious belief but a "dynamic system of knowledge" through which a "sacred world-view" is continually being constructed (Peek, *Divination Systems*, 2). These divination systems are the "primary means of articulating the epistomology of a people; . . . [they] do not simply reflect other aspects of culture; they are the means (as well as the premise) of knowing which underpins and validates all else . . . mediators especially for cultures in transition."

These systems involve a combination of "logical-analytical" and "intuitive-synthetic" modes of thinking that "in European thinking are rigidly separated" (Peek, *Divination Systems*, 3). They "shift decision-making into a liminal realm by emphatically participating in opposing cognitive modes. This may be the defining feature of divination." This "shift to the non-normal" occurs irrespective of the method used and changes the cognitive process itself (Peek, *Divination Systems*, 193). Divination valorizes this "non-normal" experience of liminal space. It engages in what archetypal psychologists have called *soul-making*.

These systems are often sponsored by an animal trickster figure, a "rival creator" whose "potent paraverbal enigmas" offer a "recurring alternative to more public, legalistic truth or clear definitions" (Shaw, *Divination Systems*, 140–141). The imaginative "assertion of a different possible world" enacts a "therapeutic cosmogony." Its "performative efficacy" continually restructures and restores the social world through individual transformation (Fernandez, *Divination Systems*, 218–219).

In archaic Greek culture, behind this portrait of a "live" divination system was diffused what Lain Entralgo has called a "pre-rational verbal therapy."[26] Its charms, enchantments, spells, hymns, secret words, and secret rituals (*epôdê, thêlkterion, kêlêma, paiêôn, apporrêta, teletai*) represented a cure of the soul, later rationalized by philosophers into the act of philosophy itself. These verbal formulae bind and loosen; they use persuasive words (*peitho*) to oppose force (*bia*) and blind necessity (*anankê*; in later thought *heimarmene*, the "compulsion of the stars").[27] These spells "produce a real and effective change in the mind of one upon whom they act" (Lain Entralgo, 120). Through their use, a liminal space opens where violent emotional states, dreams, diseases—encounters with the force of the Gods—are turned into psychic awareness. This is the "leading-out" of the soul (*psychagôgia*); and the proper cleansing agent (*katharmos*) for confusion and compulsion is the spell (*epôdê*) or oracular word (Lain Entralgo, 135). This active agent of the practice of divination engenders a peace in the psyche (*sôphrosynê*) which is the double of the order and beauty of the cosmos (Lain Entralgo, 137). The goal of divination underlies the goal of philosophy: a purification of the soul (*katharsis tês psychês*) which "saves the reality of the Gods" and enables one to understand the intelligence (*nous*) that is given by them to humans (Lain Entralgo, 128).

There are two words in English for what the Greeks called *mantike* and the Romans *divinatio*. Oracle refers to: the shrine consecrated to a God, the space set off for contact; the priest, medium, or transmitter; and the words or counsel given: the *ainigma* or dark saying that links the God and the inquirer. The word comes from the Latin *orare*, to speak; its root is *or*: to pronounce a ritual formula. "Oracle" emphasizes a magical, God-producing quality in the words that ordinarily form our human community; the oracular word is an *angelos* or messenger in its *enigmatic* appearance.

Divination refers to the act of foretelling future events or revealing occult knowledge through an "alleged" divine agency. The term has strong overtones of superstition and charlatanism, yet it contains and gives a vehicle to the "divine." The word comes through Latin *divinus*, one who is inspired by *divus*: a God, what is numinous. Its Indo-European root is *deiw*: to shine; to be manifest. The dubious act of divination makes the hidden manifest, makes it "shine."

To understand divination systems, we must add a third: to symbolize. Symbolize, taken as an *active transitive verb*, refers to the act of empowering something as a symbol. The term comes from Greek *symballô, symbollon*: to encounter, to join or throw together. Its Indo-European root, *gwel*[1], connects it with: the devil and the diabolic; with emblem, parable, parole, problem; with metabolism; with "to dance" (Greek *ballizein*; English *ballet*); with an illuminating ray or beam (Greek *bolê*); and with determination or will (*boulê*), a "throwing out or forward of the mind."

The Greek word *symbollon* originally applied to the halves of a tablet that was broken when two men became "guest-friends."[28] The expression was gradually used for the engraved shells used by initiates of mystery cults in order to recognize one another, as signs of a mutual encounter with the numinous. Part of the sacramental rites, they were signs of a communion. At the same time, the term was extended to include oracles and omens, extraordinary phenomena which must be read as links to the gods. It came to include linking tokens of all kinds: military passwords, corporate insignia, wedding bands, rings guests gave at banquets or symposia as promises of payment, permits given to aliens allowing them to reside in the city.

To empower something as a symbol, to "symbolize" it, is a fundamental act of the human soul. It creates a liminal space through which one is put in contact with the "Others" behind immediate sensible reality. The simplest objects, phrases, and words can be thus empowered:

In the Mysteries of Eleusis, the priests showed as the greatest, most admirable object a blade of wheat, harvested in silence. A scrap of cloth we might throw away as a rag, hung at the end of a staff, evokes all the feeling contained in the idea of "homeland"; and two sticks that cross each other call to mind for millions of Christians the redemption of the world through the voluntary sacrifice of a God. (Goblet d'Alviella, 6)

Divinatory processes create, maintain, and evolve symbols. Images, words, and phrases are empowered as links to liminal space, continually being changed, added to, reworked, and evolved to meet the changing

needs of contacting the *lumen naturae.* The words and images are transformed into what one poet called *mots sauvages*: "wild words" divorced
from normal syntactic relations and empowered with all the cryptic allu-
sions of a crypt full of ghosts and demons. An interesting Biblical use of
the term is in *Luke* 2, 19. After the shepherds told Mary of the angels'
signs of the Saviour, she "preserved these sayings (*rhêma*), symbolizing
them (*symballô*) in her heart."

Symbolizing is a term that values, by withdrawing words and phrases
from common currency and allowing them to "flower" in the heart. The
word is empowered as *angelos*, messenger, recognizing its daimonic ability
to create a "close encounter." Just as Jung stated of fairy tales and myths,
these "symbols": "give expression to unconscious forces, and their retelling
causes these processes to come alive again and be re-collected, thereby re-
establishing the connection between conscious and unconscious" (*CW* 9ii,
§ 280).

Divination relies on this symbolizing process, on the creation, care of,
and attention to images offered as transformational agents in the creation
of liminal space. The "healing and renewing properties" of this experience
"point to the therapeutic character of the mythic background from which
this idea comes" (*CW* 9ii, § 281). In the empowering of symbols, and in
the access to liminal space that it provides, a divinatory system involves
the user with a "spirit" not cut off from psyche, a lumen naturae previous
to the splitting of psyche and spirit which produced the demonization of
the world.

TING: THE OTHER'S VESSEL

> For now the sacrificial Knife is in the hand of him who was sacrificed
> and a death is demanded of the erstwhile sacrificer.
>
> *CW* 15, § 95

The *I Ching* or *Chou I*[29] is a fundamental text of traditional Chinese
culture. It represents a process of knowing that has been continually elaborated for almost 3,000 years antithetical to modern positivism. Its oldest
texts date back to a time when the roots of divinatory science were emerging from shamanism.[30] In the words of Richard Wilhelm, whose "scriptural" translation[31] first made the "divinatory power of the *I Ching*" (*CW*
15, § 78) available to Westerners:

Nearly all that is significant in the three thousand years of Chinese cultural history
has either taken its inspiration from this book or has exerted an influence on the
interpretation of its texts . . . not only the philosophy of China but its science and
statecraft as well have never ceased to draw from the spring of wisdom in the *I*

Ching . . . even the commonplaces of everyday life in [traditional] China [were] saturated with its influence.[32]

The *I Ching* is perhaps the oldest and most complex divinatory system surviving the occultation of the psyche and the polytheistic pre-positivist cosmos. It is one of the few oracles outside of tribal cultures which still contains a "living spirit." (*CW* 15, § 78)

Jung saw the divinatory use of the *I Ching* and its rhetoric of archetypes as a background to the emergence of Western psychology (*CW* 18, § 139). This perception was at the heart of his elaboration of "synchronicity" as an irrational connecting factor compensating the one-sidedness of causality. He perceived that the *I Ching* was the basis of an Eastern science with psychological premises radically different from Western rationalism (*CW* 15, § 80). Its language of dreams, myths, and alchemical symbols sociologists now call "primary process;" it presents a "formidable psychological system that endeavours to organize the play of the archetypes, the *mirabiles naturae operationes*, . . . so that a reading becomes possible" (*CW* 14, § 401). This divinatory system gave the user access to the archetypal energies at work in his or her situation. It linked the users to their images.

In order to know the life of the psyche and its images in this context, Jung insisted that "we have to remember the Gods of antiquity" (*CW* 9ii, § 79). These ancient Gods image living forces through which the psyche creates reality each day (*CW* 6, § 78). To come to grips with the problem of individuality, of the "Self," we must enter the *shadow* cast by the figure of Christ, the "dark and formless void" created by the Church Fathers (*CW* 9ii, § 79). Jung's concern with the Hellenistic Mystery Cults and the *daimones*, his own "initiation" during the long "fallow period" of his fantasies,[33] and his involvement with alchemical symbolism all form part of a life-long attempt to darken the Christ-figure, to enter its shadow.[34] He felt he would thus "dream the myth onward"[35] through its pagan shadow and the mystery of psyche, daimon, and cosmos. Finding, experiencing, elaborating this shadowy "psychic connection" was, for Jung, the fundamental ethical act.

The sense of history that Jung entertains here links the divinatory power of the *I Ching* and the "spirit of *tao*" he found in Chinese philosophy with the West's own "pre-scientific psychology." Use of the *I Ching* enters Jung's imagination through the *shadow* side of Western tradition: pre-Socratic philosophers, Gnostics, alchemists, theurgic magicians, Neo-platonists, astrologers, diviners, mediums, Paracelsus, Agrippa—all part of an occulted worldview which "underlies all the magical and mantic procedures that have played an important part in man's life since the remotest times" (*CW* 8, § 939–40). The "living spirit of the East" incarnate in the *I Ching* (*CW* 15, § 78) brings back to life a way of thought, an "occult science," outlawed in the West since late antiquity: something "almost taboo, outside the scope of our judgments" (*CW* 15, § 80); lingering in the "twilight" of Christian culture (*CW* 15, § 85), in "our own darkness" (*CW* 15, § 88), "something in *us* that is in need of further development" (*CW* 15, § 86).

"In the divinatory power of the *I Ching*," Jung remarked, we have "an Archimedean point from which our Western attitude of mind can be lifted off its foundations."[36] This is "capable of working a fundamental change in our view of the world" (*CW* 15, § 78). As an occult search for individual "meaning," which is Wilhelm's translation (*der Sinn*) of the Chinese term *tao*, this "could be a dangerous infection, but it might also be a remedy" for the "arrogance and tension of the European will" (*CW* 15, § 90).

The divinatory use of the *I Ching* points to the shadow because its "living spirit" is the shadow of Christianity, positivism, and rationalism: the *lumen naturae*. Use of its images re-creates the old connection: individual, daimon, psyche, cosmos. It *re-activates* this way of knowing, dimming the bright light of conscious will, directing energy to the "complexes" or daimones.

In this context, Jung saw the oracle technique of the *I Ching* as "a method of exploring the unconscious" (*CW* 11, § 966). A "collection of archaic magic spells," this "age-old oracle technique" (*CW* 11, § 999) leads the user into a liminal "dreamlike atmosphere" (*CW* 11, § 1003), a world of masks, spirit symbols, spells, and *scintillae*, which images the psyche itself.

These masks and magic spells give access to the forces which create synchronicity: the "qualities or basic conditions" of time which are "capable of manifesting themselves . . . by means of an acausal parallelism" (*CW* 15, § 81). Traditionally, they form the "living soul" of the book, "spiritual agencies . . . acting in a mysterious way, that make the yarrow-stalks give a meaningful answer" (*CW* 11, § 975). The projection of subjective contents into the oracle's symbols is an integral part of the procedure, for the masks and magic spells of this "dreamlike" system *translate* the inquirer's concerns into the language of the liminal. This creates a gap, a *kairos*, a "dragon hole" in time where the intervention of unconscious contents can change the inquirer's universe of thought, "shifting the cognitive process." Both conscious and unconscious are moved in their dynamic interchange. The energetic relation between them is adjusted, and *shen ming*, "bright spirit" or "light of the Gods," emerges. It is the experience of this way of knowing, more than any specific counsel, that is the goal of the process.

The image of the *I Ching* in Jung's own imagination, constellated when he posed a question to the oracle which would be answered in *propria persona*, was Hexagram 50, *Ting*, the Vessel (*CW* 11, § 982). It is the image of an elaborately crafted and decorated cast bronze vessel used to cook food offered to humans, to ancestral spirits, and to the Gods, thus linking the worlds through ritual procedures. The term *ting* also includes the idea of holding and containing; and the texts of the hexagram interconnect "symbolizing" or creating symbols (*hsiang*), with "cooking" (*jen*), "presenting" (*hsiang*), the "ground's fire" (*sun huo*), and "understanding brightness" (*ts'ung ming*). For Jung, the book was:

a vessel in which sacrificial offerings are brought to the gods, ritual food for their nourishment. It conceives of itself as a cult object serving to provide spiritual nourishment for the unconscious elements or forces . . . to give these forces the attention they need in order to play their part in the life of the individual. Indeed this is the original meaning of the word *religio*—a careful observation and taking account of (from *relegere*) the numinous. (CW 11, § 982)

THE NAME OF THE BOOK[37]

The central concern of the *I Ching* links it to those moments in life when one faces the encounter with an "alien" through a personal crisis or conflict. This is expressed by the key term *i*, from which the book derives its oracular function. The second term, *ching*, is an honorific for classical or canonical books, such as the *Shih Ching* or *Classic of Songs* or the *Shu Ching*, the *Classic of Documents*. *Ching* refers to: book, classic; a channel, to pass through; the warp of a fabric; constant, a standard. The *I Ching* is the classic, constant, channel, or loom of *i*. It was the first *Classic* established in Chinese culture; it points to the importance of divination as a symbolic base for poetry, history, philosophy, as well as individual conduct.

I can only be understood in terms of three other key themes in the human world: *tao, te, chün tzu*. *Tao*, literally "way," is a central term in most Eastern thought. It refers to the "way" of dynamic interaction of microcosm and macrocosm, a "way" of seeing that describes all phenomena in terms of an ongoing process and the course it traces. Thus, it is the way *in which* everything happens and the way *on which* everything happens. *Te*, often translated as power or virtue, refers to the process of *actualizing-tao*, realizing *tao* in individual life and action. It suggests a straightening of the inner essence which permits a being to become what it is intrinsically meant to be. The *chün tzu*, a term first used to describe those who wished to rise in the feudal aristocracy, refers to the ideal user of the book. A *chün tzu* is someone who strives to conform to his inherent destiny as a specific manifestation of *tao*. One is a *chün tzu* insofar as one organizes one's life according to *tao* rather than to willful intentions: to perceive, accept, and manifest one's fate. *I* is the tool of the *chün tzu* in actualizing (*te*) his identity through adaptation to the continually changing path or *tao*.

The term *i* emphasizes mobility, openness, fluidity. It refers to: change; easy, not difficult; light as the opposite of heavy; to deal lightly with, at ease; and, conversely: done without care, remiss, indifferent to, negligent. The ideogram has several possible lines of origin. Small seal characters seem to represent a lizard or a chameleon. Bronze inscriptions show the graph for sun and the graph for negative; oracle bone characters show the crescent moon and three diagonal rays. The bronze vessel inscriptions also show *i* used as a transfer character for *hsi*: gift, grant; to confer something on someone. These meanings are not contradictory, but converge on a kind of "change" that passes through the lunar and is a gift to humans. *I* implies a fluid identity. It suggests the ability to change direction quickly and radically, a flexible many-sidedness, and the use of a variety of talents to mirror the variety of being. The most adequate English translation of this term is *versatility*, the ability to remain available to the unforeseen demands of time, fate, and *tao*. This term interweaves the *i* of the cosmos, the *i* of the book, and the *i* of one who uses it to manifest *tao*.

As "easy," *i* also refers to the fact that the yarrow-stalk oracle with its texts and figures was much easier to use than the ritual pyromancy involved in ancient China's other oracle system: consulting the cracks produced in specially prepared tortoise shells when a heated bronze rod was applied to them. It was this "easy" quality of access that led to the use of this oracle by individuals outside of an established ruling class.

A discussion between King Wen and a disaffected Shang prince highlights another connection between *i* and breakdown and flux. King Wen was spiritual father of the Chou Dynasty (c. 1000–480 B.C.E.) who had spent several years in prison during the final decadence of the preceding Shang Dynasty (c. 1520–1030 B.C.E.). The discussion is taken from the *Shu Ching* or *Book of Documents*.

[King Wen] said: What the king scrutinizes is the year, the dignitaries and noblemen the months, the many lower officials the days. When in years, months, days, the season [the measure] has no *i*, the many cereals ripen, the administration is enlightened, talented men of the people are distinguished, the house is peaceful and at ease. When in days, months, years, the season has *i*, the many cereals do not ripen, the administration is dark and unenlightened, talented men of the people are in petty positions, the house is not at peace.[38]

I is not the orderly change of the seasons and generations (*hua*), nor is it the transformation (*pien*) of life into death and death into life, although it may include these types of change. *I* originates in and is a way of dealing with "trouble." It articulates the possible responses to fate, necessity, calamity, or that which "crosses" your path.

The actual name of the book is *Chou I*, that is, the *i* or versatility of Chou, distinguishing this book from other ancient oracle systems concerned with *i*. Historically, *Chou* is the name of the dynasty that ruled China in varying forms from the eleventh to about the fourth century B.C.E. So *Chou I* refers to *i*, versatility, as used by the Kings of Chou, the Chou Dynasty's versatility-book, which enabled them to be aware of and adapt to the moving universe.

The term *chou* can be imagined in another way, however, for it keeps its intrinsic meaning even when used as a proper name. Intrinsically, *chou* means extending everywhere, making a circuit, universal. It suggests both the exhaustive nature of *i* and its continual return to itself. This intrinsic meaning may be rendered as *encompassing*. As the second-century author Cheng Hsüan stated, the term *chou* refers to the book's "being all encompassing and with nothing that is not included." In the words of a contemporary sinologist, *chou* posits the book as "a formal and processual duplicate of the realm of heaven-and-earth."[39]

Thus, the concern and the aim of the book, its ethical core, might best be translated as *Encompassing Versatility*. It is an oracular text that seeks to image the individual in terms of the all-encompassing and ever-changing movement of *tao*, and the *chün tzu*'s adaptation to it through *i*, versatility.

Later philosophers articulated the implicit archaic belief that this individual adaptation also had profound social dimensions. In particular, Chu Hsi's formulation[40] of the use of the oracle became part of its greater context.

Chu Hsi argued that the user of the oracle must work his way back through the texts to the unmediated vision of the world that gave rise to the images, rather than confining himself to philosophical explanations. This is a procedure Jung would call retracing the archetypal roots. Chu Hsi felt the user was "rectified" or "clarified" in the process; the texts and figures of the *Chou I* activate the *tao-hsin* or "tao-mind" in the user, as opposed to the *jen-hsin* or "person-mind," which is frozen by literal desires. He felt that the sages who created the *i* had abstracted the dynamic patterns of Heaven-and-Earth itself in order to form the hexagrams. Thus, these texts and figures activated the inherent perfectibility of each individual. Because Chu Hsi saw the minds of the Sages, the order of Heaven-and-Earth, the *tao-hsin* in each individual, and the texts of the *i* as congruent, yarrow-stalk divination was the personal experience of listening to the "*tao-mind*" itself. Through this procedure the user did not learn about the pattern of Heaven-and-Earth, but realized it. According to Chu Hsi, this individual transformation of the person-mind into the *tao*-mind was the necessary foundation for the regeneration of the state. Self-cultivation (*hsiu-shen*) through divination led to the re-ordering of the social world (*chih-kuo*).

In positing the divinatory use of the *I Ching* as a means of individual transformation, Chu Hsi was attempting to give the ordinary person a way to break through the moral atrophy which he felt had caused the collapse of the Northern Sung Dynasty (1127 C.E.). The interiorizing process which he described connected the individual with the regenerative power inherent in the *I Ching*'s archaic origins. Chu Hsi "dreamed the myth onward" at a critical point in Chinese culture. His sense of the *I Ching*, as an individual psychological praxis which has profound social overtones, became part of the legacy of the book.

The *Classic of Change* was the basis of much of Chinese culture. Its images provided a semiotic reservoir for popular culture, for religious belief, for the most elaborate philosophical and numerological speculations. Underlying all this was the experience that the oracle is "continuous with the causal conditions in the all-under-heaven," describing the seeds of events in the world and in the human heart. Thus, it is a "mysterious and potent duplicate of that which is numinous" (Peterson, "Connective Concepts," 228–230). In this context, the *I Ching*'s "magic spells" are healing images, links to regenerating forces in the *anima mundi*, the soul of the world. Work with these "magic spells" is also a healing of the images themselves, re-constituting the occulted third world of the psyche.

VOCATUS ATQUE NON VOCATUS DEUS ADERIT

> I became acutely aware that what a child wanted to do most of all was to make a world in which to find a place to discover a self.
>
> Edith Cobb[41]

The *I Ching* consists of a set of oracular images, what the Greeks called *ainigma* or dark sayings. These texts are organized and displayed through a system of 64 six-line figures or *kua*, usually translated as *hexagrams*: all the possible combinations of six whole (———) and/or opened (— —) lines. It is these lines which are produced by the random consultative process. Each divinatory hexagram, along with the texts it displays, is thought to double a configuration of time, a cluster of dynamic imagery which shapes experience and perception. These texts and figures provide a rhetoric of the archetypes, a vocabulary of the possible modes of being and change. The process of consultation, what the normative mind sees as chance or accident, is empowered as a symbolic occurrence, a linking of the literal and the imaginal. Use of this system represents religion at its most fundamental level: attention to the psychic images that trigger, coordinate, and transform what we call "instinct" (*CW* 14, § 602–3).

As Heraclitus said of Greek pronouncements, the oracle neither speaks nor hides, it *signifies* (*sêmainei*).[42] The oracle's "signifiers" are complex clusters of meaning similar to dream-images which disfigure everyday language. Its symbolizing enacts a deliteralizing of language and events that moves the inquirer toward mysterious depths. Hellmut Wilhelm called the basic units of meaning in the oracle-texts of the *I Ching* "image-concepts"; simultaneous clusters of image and idea that unite what we normally experience as disparate qualities of mind.[43] Chinese poet-philosopher Chuang-tzu (c. 370–300 B.C.E.) would call them "wild-words," "goblet-words," "non-words," weirs or "fish-traps" for *tao*.[44]

The oracle offers not an answer but a connection, a map of the inquirer's situation as it is constellated in the psyche. To do this, it transforms words into autonomous clusters of image, force-fields indicating the presence of *daimones*, spirits, Gods. As Jung realized, far from having left these Gods behind:

Modern man has rejected only their verbal spectres, not the psychic facts. . . . The Gods have become diseases producing curious specimens for the doctor's consulting room or disordering the brains of politicians and journalists who unwittingly let loose psychic epidemics on the world. . . . Instead of allowing himself to be convinced once more that the daemon is an illusion, [modern man] ought to experience once more the reality of this illusion. (*CW* 13, § 54–55)

Oracle language reveals the "god in the disease," the daimonic presence constellated in the *kairos*, the critical moment, represented by the inquirer's question.

Two terms from the *Hsi Tz'u Chuan*[45] [a treatise forming part of the *Ten Wings* which were appended to the hexagram texts in the Han Dynasty (206 B.C.E.–220 C.E.)] expand on this process. These terms and the oral interpretive tradition that lies behind them came from the Warring States period (c. 400–220 B.C.E.),[46] a period of political conflict in China that also gave rise to the fundamental Taoist and Confucian texts. It was during this period that a more individual use of the yarrow-stalk oracle began.

According to this commentary, the function of the *i* is to provide symbols (*hsiang*; B3. 1). *I* has in it the course traced by the ongoing process (*tao*) of heaven, earth and humans (B10. 2–4; Peterson, 89), and it makes numinous (*shen*) that conduct which is imaginatively potent (A9. 18; Peterson, 104–5). In itself still and unmoving (A10. 15), when stimulated by consultation, *i* produces an echo which comprehends all causes in the realm of all-under-heaven (A10. 16; Peterson, 106), reaching the depths and grasping the seeds (A10. 18). The shamans and sages who created its symbols drummed and danced in order to bring out the spirits or *shen* (A12. 13; Peterson, 107). In the same way, these symbols speak to the unconscious mind of the inquirer, evoking an imaginative process which "completes the ceaseless activity of heaven" (Schultz, 186). The *chün tzu*, the ideal user of the book, immerses himself in the *i* and its symbols, observing the figure obtained through divination and taking joy in its words. By turning and rolling these words in his heart (A2. 10–11), he allows them to symbolize (*hsiang*) his situation, to make his situation symbolic. In this way, too, he brings out and fulfills spirit or *shen* (A12. 13; Schultz, 186).

Hsiang, symbol/to symbolize, empowers an image as archetypal, imputes to it the power to evoke a meaningful cluster of associations which connects the visible and the invisible. The term refers to: figure, form, image, likeness; configuration, pattern; the shape things take; auguries, portents, omens; to give shape to, to create an image, to represent; to imitate; acting, playing; a model, a rule, to take as a rule; the written symbol or ideogram; and the figures of the *I Ching*.

This term describes the process of creating an imaginal or liminal world. It brings together an objective figure which is part of the phenomenal world; a sign that duplicates its potency; bringing such a shape or pattern into existence; a state of mind we might call "imaginative induction"; and the symbols and figures of the *I Ching*. When one consults the oracle, one re-produces the originating act of symbolizing and becoming a symbol. Consultation affords a "crack" in time through which an imaginative world is perceived.

To do this is called *shen*, which refers to spirit, spirits, what is numinous, spiritually potent. The oracle was symbolized or empowered (*hsiang*) to further *shen* and to create *shen-ming*, bright spirit or the light of the Gods. This term links the yarrow-stalks, the means of consulting the oracle which are described as *shen* things (A11. 26), to what is mysterious, numinous, outside of and prior to literal definition; "spiritual clarity"; the spirits, *shen* or *daimones* who made the symbols of the *i* appear in the Sage-mind and who are re-created by their re-appearance; genius, vital energy, the ruling power of the personality; making or becoming a God; nameless, sacred.

Like the shamans and sage-kings of old, this treatise maintains, the one who uses the *i*'s symbolizing power re-creates the numinous world, acquiring helping-spirit, a *shen*. (A9. 19; Peterson, 105/107). The *i* is not itself a *daimon*; it is a maker of *daimones*, an imaginative discipline that allows its users to experience a *daimon* within themselves, an in-forming and regulating force. Helping-spirit, like the *lumen naturae* of alchemy, builds shapes in the psychic cosmos, peoples the inner world "from the power of the word" (*CW* 8, § 391). Creating this symbolic reality can have a synchronous effect on both individual and the world; can produce an epiphanic experience of that golden age when the Gods and humans were at one. The oracle exists as a dynamic field of meaning between user and text, a field of meaning that is continually evolving, re-created in each consultation through the archetypal mystery of its symbols.

Jung had a motto carved in stone over the door to his city house in Küsnacht: *Vocatus atque non vocatus Deus aderit*. Adopted by Jung as a psychological maxim, this is a Latin translation of the answer to a question put to Apollo's Pythia at Delphi. The Spartans asked the Oracle if Apollo would help them in their war against imperialist Athens. "Called or not called, the God will be there" expresses more than a foreknowledge of the defeat of the Athenians. It insists on the belief that the Gods intervene in human life to shape events and punish *hubris*.

Jung's use of this oracular response represents a cluster of interwoven meanings. It associates depth psychology; a critical moment or *kairos* which gives rise to a question; the Gods; an oracular sense of the unseen; the historic layers of culture and psyche; and words, speech, language. Called or uncalled, summoned or unsummoned, the Gods will be there. It is the recognition of and talking to this unseen world which is the therapeutic act *par excellence*, the heart of mythopoetic psychology. It is also the central mystery of the ancient science of divination: "not to learn something, but experience something and be set right."[47]

Jung's experience of the *daimon*, to which much of his psychological work bears witness, is an important context for the *Classic of Change* and the act of divination in modern culture, both East and West. We see this in his continual engagement with the conflict between normative concept and psychic image, in his re-discovery of the shadowy realm of the *daimones*, and in his constant elaboration of *esse in anima*, being in soul. It connects daimonic intelligence, the subversive language of the oracle, and the individual's need to re-imagine a world in which to experience a self.

This language continues to haunt us as ego and intellect confront image and God in the crisis of the *kairos*. "Haunt," "ghost," "Geist," "spook," and "phantom" are proper words to describe this under-worldly doubling. The language of psyche and oracle is threatening, for it exposes the normative ego to a numinous world it has not only ignored but attempted to destroy. *Vocatus atque non vocatus Deus aderit*: Called or not called the God will be here. As Jung often remarked, dialogue with the unseen marks the difference between serving a God and being the victim of a mania. The *I Ching* is a fundamental tool in opening the dialogue.

NOTES

1. Literally, the "disturber" or "disrupter" is God. Shortly before his death, Jung elaborated on this long-held belief, which often came up in his conversation and practice: "To this day God is the name by which I designate all things which cross my wilful path violently and recklessly, all things which upset my subjective views, plans and intentions and change the course of my life for better or for worse." C. G. Jung, interview in *Good Housekeeping*, December 1961; quoted in Edward Edinger, *Ego and Archetype* (New York: C. G. Putnam, 1972), p. 101.

2. John Milton, *Paradise Lost*, iv, 75; *Collected Works*, ed. Helen Darbishire, 2 vols. (Oxford: Oxford University Press, 1952–1955). All further references are to this edition.

3. "Le Poète se fait *voyant* par un long, immense et raisonné *dérèglement de tous les sens*. Toutes les formes d'amour, de souffrance, de folie; il cherche lui-meme, il epuise en lui tous les poisons . . . il devient entre tous le grand malade, le grand criminel, le grand maudit—et le supreme Savant—car il arrive a l' *inconnu*!" Letter to Paul Demeny (15 May 1871); Arthur Rimbaud, *Oeuvres*, ed. S. Bernard and A. Guyaux (Paris: Bordas, Classiques Garnier, 1991), p. 348.

4. CW 9i, § 40; references to Jung's *Collected Works* (CW) are to Bollingen Series XX, vols. 1–20, trans. R. F. C. Hull (Princeton, NJ: Princeton University Press, 1957–1979).

5. William Butler Yeats, "The Second Coming"; *Collected Poems* (London: Macmillan, 1952).

6. Word definitions throughout the chapter are drawn from the *Oxford English Dictionary* (Oxford: Clarendon Press, 1971) and *The American Heritage Dictionary of the English Language* (Boston: Houghton Mifflin, 1980). Contexts for Greek terms come from H. G. Liddell and R. Scott, *A Greek-English Lexicon* (Oxford: Oxford University Press, 1973). Further contexts for Greek and philosophical terms are drawn from R. B. Onians, *The Origins of European Thought* (Cambridge: Cambridge University Press, 1951; rpt. 1988) and F. E. Peters, *Greek Philosophical Terms: A Historical Lexicon* (New York: New York University Press, 1967).

7. Evidence for and re-construction of Indo-European root-syllables are found in Julius Pokorny, *Indo-germanisches Etymologisches Wörterbuch* (Bern, 1959). An explanatory essay and shorter index are contained in *The American Heritage Dictionary of the English Language*, pp. 1496–1550. Russell A. Lockhart, *Words as Eggs* (Dallas: Spring Publications, 1983) is an interesting consideration of the use of these "seed-syllables" in therapeutic work.

8. See James Hillman, *The Dream and the Underworld* (New York: Harper and Row, 1979), p. 14ff.

9. *Ethos anthrôpôi daimon*; I follow Jung and Hillman here in seeing Heraclitus as a "father" of depth psychology rather than a champion of rationalism. Numbering of the fragments is from Diels-Kranz, English translation by K. Freeman, *Ancilla to the Pre-Socratic Philosophers* (Oxford: B. H. Blackwell, 1948). Other translations consulted are G. S. Kirk and J. E. Raven, *The Pre-Socratic Philosophers* (Cambridge: Cambridge University Press, 1963) and M. Marcovitch, *Heraclitus: Greek Text with Short Commentary* (Merida, Venezuela: Los Andes University Press, 1967). See also F. M. Cornford, *From Religion to Philosophy* (New York: Harper and Row, 1957); W. K. C. Guthrie, *A History of Greek Philosophy*, vol. 1 (Cambridge: Cambridge University Press, 1962); and P. Wheelwright, *Heraclitus* (Princeton, NJ: Princeton University Press, 1959).

10. See R. L. Fox, *Pagans and Christians* (New York: Alfred Knopf, 1987), pp. 608–662; and A. H. Armstrong, "Itineraries in Late Antiquity," *Eranos 56* (1987): 105–132. *In hoc signo vinces* (in this sign you conquer) is the motto associated with Constantine's conversion to Christianity immediately preceding his decisive victory in the Battle of Ponte Milvio, 312 C.E. This victory made him the first Christian emperor. On the day before the battle he saw a "vision" of a cross in the sky, and that night dreamed of a shining figure who ordered him to inscribe the heavenly sign on his soldiers' shields.

Constantine's conversion and victory put the government in the hands of Christian bishops who "grabbed the new wealth and power with both hands" (Armstrong, "Itineraries in Late Antiquity," 119). Constantine filled the bureaucracy with their followers, creating a new class, the "aristocracy of service." He exempted Christian clergy from civic duties and taxes, and endowed the largest construction project undertaken in Antiquity, a string of great churches running from Rome to the Holy Land. The pagan oracles were closed, the temples and their wealth taken over. In a master stroke of allegorical re-interpretation, the major texts of pagan poetry, religion, and philosophy were defined as foretelling the advent of Christ who represents their "true" meaning. This allegorical interpretation was announced by Constantine himself in a speech on Good Friday, 325 C.E. (Fox, *Pagans and Christians*, 643–653). It became a major tool used by Christian thinkers to preempt the pagan "way of knowing." Thus, *in hoc signo vinces* became an imaginal as well as a literal motto.

11. See Peter Brown, *The World of Late Antiquity* (London: Thames and Hudson, 1971); E. R. Dodds, *Pagan and Christian in an Age of Anxiety* (Cambridge: Cambridge University Press, 1956); Fox, *Pagans and Christians*; A. J. Festugiere, *Personal Religion among the Greeks* (Berkeley: University of California Press, 1954); and A. H. Armstrong, "Itineraries in Late Antiquity."

12. The Greek term *kosmos* links "order" with "ornament" and "intelligence." The visible world (*kosmos aisthêtôs*), which is the "visible God" (*horatos theos*), is in constant mimetic interaction with the "intelligible world" (*kosmos noêtos*). Image, intelligence, and spirit are not in rivalry in *kosmos*. Jung perceived that this "sacred cosmos" was the equivalent of the psyche itself. See Jean Pépin, "Cosmic Piety," in *Classical Mediterranean Spirituality*, vol. 15 of *World Spirituality* (New York: Crossroads, 1986), pp. 408–435.

13. This is elaborated in particular in Paul's *Epistle to the Romans*, which formed the basis of later Christian theory culminating in Augustine's *De Civitate Dei*. I refer throughout to the *Revised Standard Version of the Bible* as seen through the Greek-English Concordances: John Ellison, ed., *Nelson's Complete Concordance of the Revised Standard Version of the Bible* (New York: Thomas Nelson and Sons, 1957); *Greek-English Lexicon of the New Testament* (New York: United Bible Societies, 1988–1989); and *Theological Dictionary of the New Testament*, ed. G. Kittel (Grand Rapids, MI: Eerdmans, 1964).

14. Peter Brown, *Body and Society* (New York: Columbia University Press, 1988), p. 27. Also, from Franz Cumont, The *Mysteries of Mithra* (cited CW 5, § 109):

> The gods were everywhere, and they mingled in all the events of daily life. The fire that cooked the food and warmed the bodies of the faithful, the water that allayed their thirst and cleansed them, the very air they breathed, and the light that shone for them, all were objects of their adoration. . . . When the initiate betook himself in the evening to the sacred grotto concealed in the solitude of the forest, at every step new sensations awakened in his heart some mystical emotion. The stars that shone in the sky, the wind that whispered in the foliage, the spring or brook that hastened murmuring to the valley, even the earth which he trod under his feet, were in his eyes divine, and all surrounding nature evoked in him a worshipful fear of the infinite forces that swayed the universe.

See too A. H. Armstrong, "The Ancient and Continuing Pieties," in *Classical Mediterranean Spirituality*, (vol. 15 of *World Spirituality* (New York: Crossroads, 1986).

15. *Daimon*, god, archetype, and hero are not clearly demarcated terms in Mediterranean culture; they describe different aspects of the same experience. Even careful philosophical analysts like Plotinus mix the terms; see Stephen MacKenna, Plotinus' *The Enneads* (London: Faber, 1956), p. xxvi. The gods may be said to represent "the deepest patterns of psychic functioning, the roots of the soul governing the perspectives we have of ourselves and the world": James Hillman, *Revisioning Psychology* (New York: Harper and Row, 1975), p. xiii. *Daimon* is God or the gods as they impinge directly on the individual, constituting that individual's fate as transformational *energia*.

16. See C. A. Patrides, "The Cessation of the Oracles: The History of a Legend," *PMLA* 60, 4 (1963): 500–507; and James Hillman, *Pan and the Nightmare* (New York: Spring Publications, 1972), particularly p. li. On the myth that Christ had forever closed the doors to the Underworld, see F. Huidekoper, *The Belief of the First Three Centuries Concerning Christ's Mission to the Underworld* (New York: James Miller, 1876); and James Hillman, *The Dream and the Underworld*, chapter 4 on "Barriers" and "Peaks and Vales," in *Puer Papers* (Dallas: Spring Publications, 1989).

17. In Christian myth, Lucifer (literally "light-bearer") became a rebel archangel whose fall from heaven was referred to in *Isaiah* 14, 42: "How thou art fallen, oh day-star, son of the morning." This Old Testament passage, part of a polemic against the King of Babylon, was interpreted to mean that the chief of the angels who "kept not their estate" was named Lucifer before he fell, and thereafter Satan, the Adversary. This Lucifer was identified with *Phosphoros* and the *Phosphoroi*, pagan terms which referred both to the "morning and evening star" and to a particular shining or revealing quality associated with the gods prior to the Olympian cults. Thus, Hestia's hearthfire, Hermes' wayfinding, Artemis' knowledge of the wilds, Hekate's dark wisdom, Selene's shining, Persephone's underworld knowing, Pan's spontaneity, and Aphrodite's beauty were all a quality of "*phosphoros*." See W. H. Roscher, *Lexikon der Griechischen und Römischen Mythologie* (Leipzig, 1902–1909; rpt. Hildesheim: Georg Olms Verlag, 1978), III.2, entry "*phosphoroi/phosphoros*." It was this identification that allowed Christian apologists to maintain with Augustine, that "*Omnes dii gentium daemona/all the gods of the pagans are demons*" (*Enn. Psal.*, Ps 96, PL xxxvi, 1231–1232) and that these demons are the devil. Thus, they turned Lucifer into Satan, the adversary of Jahweh, the Old Testament God. Another often-used passage was *Genesis* 6 in which the "sons of God" who were set over men "fell" by copulating with the "daughters of men," thus producing a race of demons. These too were identified with the pagan Gods (Justin, 2 *Apol*, 128; see *Encyclopedia of Religion and Ethics*, ed. James Hastings, 12 vols. [Edinburgh: T&T Clark, 1908–1921], entry "demons and spirits: Christian.") All of these demons were seen to occupy themselves particularly with the divination and magic which was their "light" (Augustine, *c. Academ.*, i, 19, 20).

18. In alchemical terms, *lumen naturae* is the "light of nature" as opposed to the *numen* of spiritual revelation. It is a *sol invisibilis* given to the individual, accessible through and identical with the "subtle" or "astral" body (*ôchema pneuma*). It offers each individual "sufficient predestined light that he err not" (*CW* 8, § 390; quoting Paracelsus). Phenomenologically, *lumen naturae* is experienced as *scintillaes*; sparks of the world soul scattered throughout the dark sea of night, germinal luminosities which are the seedbed of worlds to come (*mundi futuri seminarium*; *CW* 8, § 388). This natural force, also described as an underworld fire, an *ignis mercurialis*, is synonymous with the pagan *cosmos* and *aion* (*CW* 13, § 256).

19. Jung theorized about the "necessity" of Christianity on two levels. First, he speculated that the "flight from the world" had been dialectically necessary to build up a "type of thinking independent of external factors," the "sovereignty of the idea," which then entered into a new relation with Nature (*CW* 5, § 113). Thus, there existed for Jung a "golden age"; the "fantastic mythological world of the [High] Middle Ages" (*CW* 18, § 1363) when the *numen* of spiritual revelation coexisted with the *lumen* of revived pagan spirit. His fascination and identification with Paracelsus (1493–1541), a Swiss alchemical philosopher of "prescient ideas"

who could still hold the *numen* and *lumen* together, is a reflection of this (*CW* 8, § 388–393; *CW* 13, § 148, 197–200). On the Antique World in the Middle Ages see: Jean Seznec, *The Survival of the Pagan Gods*, trans. B. Sessions, (New York: Pantheon, Bollingen Series XXXIII, 1953); and Valerie Flint, *The Rise of Magic in Early Medieval Europe* (Princeton, NJ: Princeton University Press, 1991).

Second, Christianity was "a frantic and desperate attempt to create—out of no matter how doubtful material—a spiritual monarch, a *pantocrator*, in opposition to the concretized divinity of Rome" (*CW* 18, § 1568). It arose in opposition to the "whirlwinds of brutality and unchained libido that roared through the streets of Imperial Rome" (*CW* 5, § 104) and answered the "strange melancholy and longing for deliverance" of a society where 60 percent of the population were slaves (*CW* 10, § 249–250). This view was intensified by Jung's identification of the rise of the dictators with both the old German god of "storm and frenzy," Wotan (*CW* 10, "Wotan," § 371–399) and with a return to the "brutality" of Rome (*CW* 5, § 341). Jung's deeper sense of the pagan as psyche was often lost in this panic. See James Hillman, "Dionysos in Jung's Writing," *Spring* 32 (1972), pp. 191–225.

20. *Briefe III*, p. 225, 9. II. 1959; English translation in *C. G. Jung: Letters*, ed. Gerhard Adler and Aniela Jaffé, trans. R. F. C. Hull (Princeton, NJ: Princeton University Press, Bollingen Series XCV: 2, 1975). See Wolfgang Giegerich, "The Advent of the Guest: Shadow Integration and the Rise of Psychology," *Spring* 51 (1991), pp. 86–106.

21. See James Hillman, "Senex and Puer," in *Puer Papers* (Dallas: Spring Publications, 1989), p. 14. On "soulmaking," creating an imaginative cosmos, see James Hillman, *Re-visioning Psychology*, particularly pp. ix–xvii and chapter 4.

22. The Greek word is *homoioma*. It suggests: to make a likeness, to become like, to experience being "like" but not identical. According to Paul (*Romans* 1, 18–23), this is the great sin of the pagans. They hold the Spirit captive (*crateô*) in the cheating lies (*pseudo*) which are their images (*eikon*). Thus, they exchange the glory of the Lord for likeness or likening (*homoioma*). The "psychic" pagans worship and serve (*esebathêsan* kai elateusan; technical cultic terms) the creatures, abandoning the creator.

Through his use of the term *homoioma*, Paul is collapsing a "way of knowing." *Homoios* is the basis of psychological knowledge, magic, and science: that "like is known by like or likeness." The knower knows the known through a likening element between them, and in this knowing the subject becomes "like" but not identical with that which is known. It is a principle of likening to spirit (*homoiôsis theô*) for which images constitute the needed relatedness (*sympatheia*) of things. This "likening" ensouls ritual acts, divinatory processes, and mystery cults. The imaginative process evoked in *homoioma* "expresses a mystery that reaches down into the history of the human mind . . . far beyond the beginnings of Christianity. . . . Man expresses his most fundamental and most important psychological conditions in this ritual, this magic . . . the cult performance of basic psychological facts" (*CW* 18, § 616–617).

23. Cited by J. H. Matthews, *An Introduction to Surrealism* (University Park: Pennsylvania State University Press, 1967), p. 67.

24. A. Bouché-Leclercq, *Histoire de la divination dans l'antiquite*, 4 vols. (Paris, 1879; rpt. Aalen: Scientia Verlag, 1978), v. 1, pp. 1–6, my translation. See also

H. W. Parke, *Greek Oracles* (London, 1967) and R. Flaceliere, *Devins et oracles grecs* (Paris, 1961).

25. Phillip M. Peek, ed., *African Divination Systems: Ways of Knowing* (Bloomington: Indiana University Press, 1991). In the following discussion I cite: Phillip Peek, "The Study of Divination, Present and Past" (1–22) and "African Divination Systems: Non-Normal Modes of Cognition" (193–212); Roslind Shaw, "Splitting Truths from Darkness: Epistemological Aspects of Temne Divination" (137–152); and James W. Fernandez, "Afterword" (213–222). The classic study of an African tribal divination system is William Bascomb, *Ifa Divination: Communication between Gods and Men in West Africa* (Bloomington: Indiana University Press, 1969; rpt. 1991).

26. Pedro Lain Entralgo, *The Therapy of the Word in Classical Antiquity*, ed. and trans. L. J. Rather and John M. Sharp (New Haven, CT: Yale University Press, 1970), p. xviii.

27. *On peitho and ananke*, see James Hillman, "On the Necessity of Abnormal Psychology: Ananke and Athene," in *Facing the Gods* (Dallas: Spring Publications, 1980), particularly pp. 18–21. Plato maintained that the cosmos comes into being when *Nous*, the intuitive mind, persuades (*peitho*) Ananke, that is, offers her "persuasive words" (Tim. 47e–48a).

28. The following discussion is taken from Eugène Goblet d'Alviella, *La migration des symboles* (Paris, 1891), pp. 1–6, my translation. This is one of Jung's major sources.

29. The Chinese text used is *Harvard-Yenching Institute Sinological Index Series, Supplement 10: A Concordance to the Yi Ching* (rpt. Taipei: Chinese Materials and Research Aids Service Center, 1966). This reproduces, with a Concordance, the last of the "classic" editions of the text, the *Chou-I-Che-Chung* or Palace Edition of 1715. Apart from a small group of perennially contested "loan-words," the fundamental text and appendices have remained stable since the late Han Dynasty (200 B.C.E.–200 C.E.). Changes in interpretation of these mysterious texts have marked significant cultural shifts in Chinese history. The current interpretive strategy is based on *yi gu* or "scepticism toward antiquity" and is characterized by what an American practitioner has called a "ruthless literal-mindedness" (Kunst, viii). For an overview of this attitude and scholarship see Richard Kunst, *The Original Yijing: A Text, Phonetic Transcription, Translation and Indexes* (Ann Arbor, MI: University Microfilms International, 1985) which includes an extensive bibliography.

30. On the history of divinatory methods in China, see Leon Vandermeersch, "De la tortue à l'achillee," in *Divination et rationalité* (Paris: Editions du Seuil, 1974), pp. 29–51, and "The Origin of Milfoil Divination and the Primitive Form of the *I Ching*," paper presented at the Workshop on Divination and Portent Interpretation in Ancient China, University of California, Berkeley, June 20–July 1, 1983, rpt. (French) *Hexagrammes* 4 (1989), pp. 5–24; and Michael Loewe, "China," in *Oracles and Divination* (Boulder, CO: Shambhala, 1981), pp. 38–62.

31. In *The Way and its Power: A Study of the Tao Tê Ching and its Place in Chinese Thought* (London, 1934; rpt. New York: Grove Press, 1958), pp. 12–13, Arthur Waley distinguished two translation "strategies": historical and scriptural. The historical method seeks to establish what a text *meant* to certain people at a certain time. The scriptural method is concerned with what the text *means* to those who are using it in a religious or imaginative sense. Richard Wilhelm was the first

Westerner to translate a living context for the *I Ching*'s texts, in his case that of Neo-Confucianism.

32. Richard Wilhelm, *Preface* to *The I Ching or Book of Changes, The Richard Wilhelm Translation rendered into English by Cary F. Baynes* (Princeton, NJ: Princeton University Press, Bollingen Series XIX, 3rd ed., 1967, rpt. 1969), p. xlvii. Wilhelm wrote in 1923; "everyday life" in China has radically altered since then.

33. See *Analytical Psychology: Notes of the Seminar Given in 1925 by C. G. Jung*, ed. William McGuire (Princeton, NJ: Princeton University Press, Bollingen Series XCIX, 1989), pp. 22–97. Jung compared his own experience of the unconscious with the "ancient mysteries" of initiation (97–99) and later stated (*CW* 11, § 842): "the only initiation process that is still alive and practiced today in the West is the analysis of the unconscious."

34. See James Hillman, *The Dream and the Underworld*, pp. 89–90. In an early letter to Freud, Jung described his work as an attempt to:

> transform Christ back into the soothsaying god of the vine which he was, and in this way absorb those ecstatic instinctual forces of Christianity for the one purpose of making the cult and the myth what they once were—a drunken feast of joy where man regained the ethos and holiness of an animal. That was the beauty and purpose of classical religion, which from God knows what temporary biological needs has turned into a Misery Institute. Yet what infinite rapture and wantonness lies dormant in our religion, waiting to be led back to their true destination! . . . only this . . . development can serve the vital forces of religion.

The Freud-Jung Letters, ed. William McGuire (Princeton, NJ: Princeton University Press, 1974), p. 294. See also *CW* 6, § 78–93, where a more sober Jung struggles with the inherent tendency of Christianity to "paralyze" fantasy and the "specific activity of the psyche."

35. The phrase is from *CW* 9ii, § 271: "Even the best attempts at explanation [of the archetype] are only more or less successful translations into another metaphorical language. . . . The most we can do is to *dream the myth onwards* and give it a modern dress." Marie-Louise von Franz summarizes Jung's commitment to "dreaming-on" the Christian archetype in her introduction to The Zofingia Lectures (*CW* Supplementary Volume A), pp. xxiv–xxv.

36. Manfred Porkert examines this in completely different terms in "The Difficult Task of Blending Chinese and Western Science: The Case of Modern Interpretations of Traditional Chinese Medicine," *Explorations in the History of Science and Technology in China: Special Number of the "Collections of Essays on Chinese Literature and History" in Honor of the Eightieth Birthday of Dr. Joseph Needham*, ed. Li Guohao et al. (Shanghai: Chinese Classics Publishing House, 1982), pp. 553–572.

37. The following material elaborating the themes, terms, structure, and history of the *Chou Yi* is drawn from *Chou Yi: The Oracle of Encompassing Versatility*, 3 vols., *Eranos 58–1989, 59–1990*, and *60–1991* (forthcoming).

38. Bernard Karlgren, *The Book of Documents* (texts and translation), reprinted from Bulletin XXII/1950 (Stockholm: Museum of Far Eastern Antiquities, 1950), p. 33. Traditionally, the *i* was held to have been created in this "declining era" that

marked the end of the Shang and the beginning of the "bountiful potency of the Chou" (*Hsi Tz'u*, B2.1, B11.1; see note 45). In later China, identification with the early Chou rulers was a way of asserting the correctness of one's stance in an otherwise decadent age. See also Herrlee G. Creel, *The Birth of China* (New York: Ungar, 1937) and *The Origins of Statecraft in China*, vol. I, (Chicago: University of Chicago Press, 1980); and Hellmut Wilhelm, "Sacrifice in the *I Ching*," *Spring* 32 (1972): pp. 191–225, reprinted in *Heaven, Earth and Man in the Book of Changes* (Seattle: University of Washington Press, 1977). Many of the songs of the *Shih Ching* or *Book of Songs* (c. 800 B.C.E.) deal with this founding myth.

39. Willard J. Peterson, "Some Connective Concepts in China," *Eranos* 57 (1988): 225. The reference to Cheng Hsüan is taken from W. J. Peterson, "Making Connections: 'Commentary on the Attached Verbalizations' of the *Book of Change*," *Harvard Journal of Asiatic Studies* 42, 1 (June 1982): 67–116.

40. On Chu Hsi, see J. A. Adler, "Chu Hsi and Divination," in *Sung Dynasty Uses of the I Ching* (Princeton, NJ: Princeton University Press, 1990); Peter K. Bol, "Chu Hsi's Redefinition of Literati Learning," in *Neo-Confucian Reflection on the Confucian Genre* (Cambridge, MA: Harvard University Council on East Asian Studies, 1986); Wm. Theodore de Bary, *Neo-Confucian Orthodoxy and the Learning of the Mind-Heart* (New York: Columbia University Press, 1981); Wing-Tsit Chan (trans.), *Reflections on Things at Hand: The Neo-Confucian Anthology Compiled by Chu Hsi and Lu Tzu-Ch'ien* (New York: Columbia University Press, 1967); and E. A. Kracke, Jr., "Sung Society: Change within Tradition," *Far Eastern Quarterly* 14 (1954–1955): 479–88.

41. Edith Cobb, "The Ecology of the Imagination in Childhood," *Daedalus* 88 (1959): 537–548, 540.

42. Fragment 93 (Freeman). The translation of "*sêmainei*" as "signify" is mine; a more usual translation is "makes signs."

43. Hellmut Wilhelm, "The Interplay of Image and Concept in the *Book of Changes*," *Eranos* 36 (1967): 31–57, reprinted in *Heaven, Earth and Man in the Book of Changes* (op. cit.), pp. 190–222.

44. *Complete Works of Chuang-tzu*, trans. Burton Watson (New York: Columbia University Press, 1968), sections 22, 7. 27b; 27, 9. 7a; 26, 9. 6a.

45. The *Hsi Tz'u Chuan* ("Commentary on the Attached Verbalizations") or *Ta Chuan* ("Great Commentary"), makes up two of the Ten Wings added to the *Chou I* when it became a "Classic" in the Han Dynasty. Willard Peterson, "Making Connections: Commentary on the Attached Verbalizations of the *Book of Change*" (op. cit), is an excellent analysis of its basic premises, offering a brief discussion of the textual history and a new translation of selected passages. I also refer to Larry Schultz, *Lai Chih-te (1526–1604) and the Phenomenology of the Classic of Change* (Ann Arbor, MI: University Microfilms, 1982), a study of an important commentator on the *Chou I* and the *Hsi Tz'u*. The major English translation (badly outdated) is contained in the Wilhelm/Baynes *I Ching or Book of Changes* (Book II) (op. cit.); see also Gerald Swanson, *The Great Treatise: Commentary Tradition to the Book of Changes* (Ann Arbor, MI: University Microfilms, 1979). The Hsi Tz'u Chuan was "for two thousand years one of the most important statements in Chinese tradition on knowing how the cosmos worked and how humans might relate to that working" (Peterson, 67).

46. On the Warring States Period, a time of political chaos which was also the

"golden age of Chinese philosophy," see A. C. Graham, *Disputers of the Tao: Philosophical Argument in Ancient China* (La Salle, IL: Open Court, 1989).

47. Aristotle, *Select Fragments*, ed. W. D. Ross (Oxford: Clarendon, 1952), p. 87. Cited in Morton Smith, "Transformation by Burial," *Eranos* 52 (1983): 104. "Set right" translates Greek *diatithesthai*; to experience" (*pathein*) indicates involvement of the psyche, rather than simple ability to acquire information (*mathein*). See also *The Ancient Mysteries: A Sourcebook*, ed. Marvin W. Meyer, (New York: Harper and Row, 1991).

REFERENCES

Adler, Gerhard, and Aniela Jaffé (eds.). 1975. *C. G. Jung: Letters*. R. F. C. Hull, trans. Princeton, NJ: Princeton University Press.

Adler, J. A. 1990. *Sung Dynasty Uses of the I-Ching*. Princeton, NJ: Princeton University Press.

American Heritage Dictionary of the English Language. 1980. Boston: Houghton-Mifflin.

Aristotle. 1951. *Nicomachean Ethics*. H. H. Joachim, commentary; D. A. Rees, ed. Oxford: Clarendon Press.

Aristotle. 1952. *Select Fragments*. W. D. Ross, ed. Oxford: Clarendon Press.

Aristotle. 1992. *Eudemian Ethics*. Michael Woods, trans. and commentary. Oxford: Clarendon Press.

Armstrong, A. H. 1986. "Ancient and Continuing Pieties." In *Classical Mediterranean Spirituality*. New York: Crossroads.

Armstrong, A. H. 1987. "Itineraries in Late Antiquity." *Eranos* 56: 105–132.

Bascomb, William. 1969. *Ifa Divination: Communication between Gods and Men in West Africa*. Bloomington: Indiana University Press.

Bol, Peter K. 1986. *Neo-Confucian Reflection on the Confucian Genre*. Cambridge, MA: Harvard University Council on East Asian Studies.

Bouché-Leclercq, A. 1978 (rpt.). *Histoire de la divinations dans l'antiquité*. Aalen: Scientia Verlag.

Brown, Peter. 1964. *Body and Society*. Grand Rapids, MI: Eerdmans.

Brown, Peter. 1971. *The World of Late Antiquity*. London: Thames and Hudson.

Chan, Wing-Tsit (ed. and trans.). 1967. *Reflections on Things at Hand: The Neo-Confucian Anthology Compiled by Chu Hsi and Lu-Tzu-Ch'ien*. New York: Columbia University Press.

Chuang-tzu. 1968. *Complete Works*. Burton Watson, trans. New York: Columbia University Press.

Creel, Herlee G. 1937. *The Birth of China*. New York: Ungar.

Creel, Herlee G. 1980. *The Origins of Statecraft in China*. Chicago: University of Chicago Press.

d'Alviella, Eugène Goblet. 1956. *La migration des symboles*. New York: University Books.

deBary, W. T. 1981. *Neo-Confucian Orthodoxy and the Learning of the Mind-Heart*. New York: Columbia University Press.

Diels-Kranz. 1948. *Ancilla to the Pre-Socratic Philosophers*. K. Freeman, trans. Oxford: B. H. Blackwell.

Dodds, E. R. 1956. *Pagan and Christian in an Age of Anxiety*. Cambridge: Cambridge University Press.

Edinger, Edward. 1972. *Ego and Archetype*. New York: C. G. Putnam.

Ellison, John (ed.). 1957. *Nelson's Complete Concordance of the Revised Standard Version of the Bible*. New York: Nelson.

Festugiere, A. J. 1954. *Personal Religion among the Greeks*. Berkeley: University of California Press.

Flaceliere, R. 1961. *Devins et oracles Grecs*. Paris: Presses Universitaire de France.

Flint, Valerie. 1991. *The Rise of Magic in Early Medieval Europe*. Princeton, NJ: Princeton University Press.

Fox, R. L. 1987. *Pagans and Christians*. New York: Alfred Knopf.

Giegerich, Wolfgang. 1991. "The Advent of the Guest: Shadow Integration and the Rise of Psychology." *Spring* 51: 86–106.

Graham, A. C. 1989. *Disputers of the Tao: Philosophical Argument in Ancient China*. La Salle, IL: Open Court.

Hastings, James. 1921. *Encyclopedia of Religion and Ethics*. Edinburgh: T. & T. Clark.

Hillman, James. 1972a. "Dionysos in Jung's Writing." *Spring* 32: 191–225.

Hillman, James. 1972b. *Pan and the Nightmare*. Dallas, TX: Spring Publications.

Hillman, James. 1975. *Re-visioning Psychology*. New York: Harper and Row.

Hillman, James. 1979. *The Dream and the Underworld*. New York: Harper and Row.

Hillman, James. 1980. *Facing the Gods*. Dallas, TX: Spring Publications.

Hillman, James. 1989. *Puer Papers*. Dallas, TX: Spring Publications.

Hobbes, Thomas. 1851 (rpt.). *Aristotle's Treatise on Rhetoric, Literally Translated from the Greek*. London: H. G. Bohn.

Huidekoper, F. 1876. *The Belief of the First Three Centuries Concerning Christ's Mission to the Underworld*. New York: James Miller.

Jung, Carl G. 1979. *Collected Works* (abbr. *CW*). R. F. C. Hull, trans. (Bollingen Series XX). Princeton, NJ: Princeton University Press.

Karlgren, Bernard. 1950. *The Book of Documents*. Stockholm: Museum of Far Eastern Antiquities.

Kirk, G. S., and J. E. Raven. 1963. *The Pre-Socratic Philosophers*. Cambridge: Cambridge University Press.

Kittel, G. (ed.). 1964. *Theological Dictionary of the New Testament*. Grand Rapids, MI: W. B. Eerdmans.

Kracke, E. A., Jr. 1955. "Sung Society: Change within Tradition." *Far Eastern Quarterly* 14: 479–488.

Kunst, Richard. 1985. *The Original Yijing: A Text, Phonetic Transcription, Translation and Indexes*. Ann Arbor, MI: University Microfilms International.

Lain Entralgo, Pedro. 1970. *The Therapy of the Word in Classical Antiquity*. L. J. Rather and J. M. Sharp, eds. and trans. New Haven, CT: Yale University Press.

Liddell, H. G. and R. Scott. 1973. *A Greek-English Lexicon*. Oxford: Oxford University Press.

Lockhart, Russell A. 1983. *Words as Eggs*. Dallas, TX: Spring Publications.

Loewe, Michael. 1981. "China." In *Oracles and Divination*. Boulder, CO: Shambhala.

Louw, J. P. (ed.). 1988–1989. *Greek-English Lexicon of the New Testament*. New York: United Bible Societies.

McGuire, William (ed.). 1974. *The Freud-Jung Letters*. Princeton, NJ: Princeton University Press.

McGuire, William (ed.). 1989. *Analytical Psychology: Notes of the Seminar Given in 1925 by C. G. Jung*. Princeton, NJ: Princeton University Press.

MacKenna, Stephen. 1956. *Plotinus' Enneads*. London: Faber.

Marcovitch, M. 1967. *Heraclitus: Greek Text with Short Commentary*. Merida, Venezuela: Los Andes University Press.

Matthews, J. H. 1967. *An Introduction to Surrealism*. University Park: Pennsylvania State University Press.

Meyer, Marvin W. (ed.). 1991. *The Ancient Mysteries: A Sourcebook*. New York: Harper and Row.

Milton, John. 1955. *Paradise Lost*. In *Collected Works*. Helen Darbishire, ed. Oxford: Oxford University Press.

Onians, R. B. 1988. *The Origins of European Thought*. Cambridge: Cambridge University Press.

Oxford English Dictionary. 1971. Oxford: Clarendon Press.

Parke, H. W. 1967. *Greek Oracles*. London: Hutchinson.

Patrides, C. A. 1963. "The Cessation of the Oracles: The History of a Legend." *PMLA* 60(4): 500–507.

Peek, Phillip M. (ed.). 1991. *African Divination Systems: Ways of Knowing*. Bloomington: Indiana University Press.

Pepin, Jean. 1986. "Cosmic Piety." In *Classical Mediterranean Spirituality*. New York: Crossroads.

Peters, F. E. 1967. *Greek Philosophical Terms: A Historical Lexicon*. New York: New York University Press.

Peterson, Willard J. 1982. "Making Connections: 'Commentary on the Attached Verbalizations' of the *Book of Change*." *Harvard Journal of Asiatic Studies* 42(1): 67–116.

Peterson, Willard J. 1988. "Some Connective Concepts in China." *Eranos* 57: 225.

Plato. 1961. *Collected Dialogues*. Edith Hamilton & Huntington Cairns, eds. Princeton, NJ: Princeton University Press.

Plato. 1984. *Laws*. R. G. Bury, trans. Cambridge, MA: Harvard University Press.

Pokorny, Julius. 1959. *Indo-germanisches Etymologisches Wörterbuch*. Bern: A. Francke Verlag.

Porkert, Manfred. 1982. "The Difficult Task of Blending Chinese and Western Science." In *Explorations in the History of Science and Technology in China*. Li Guohao et al., eds. Shanghai: Chinese Classics Publishing House.

Rimbaud, Arthur. 1991. Letter to Paul Demeny (15 May 1871). In *Oeuvres*. S. Bernard and A. Guyuax, eds. Paris: Bordas, Classiques Garnier.

Roscher, W. H. 1978. *Lexikon der Griechischen und Römischen Mythologie*. Rpt. Hildesheim: Georg Olms Verlag.

Schultz, Larry. 1982. *Lai Chih-te (1526–1604) and the Phenomenology of the Classic of Change*. Ann Arbor, MI: University Microfilms International.

Seznec, Jean. 1953. *The Survival of the Pagan Gods*. B. Sessions, trans. New York: Pantheon.

Smith, Morton. 1983. "Transformation by Burial." *Eranos* 52: 104.

Strauss, Leo. 1975. *The Argument and the Action of Plato's Laws*. Chicago: University of Chicago Press.

Swanson, Gerald. 1979. *The Great Treatise: Commentary Tradition to the Book of Changes*. Ann Arbor, MI: University Microfilms International.

Vandermeersch, Leon. 1974. *Divination et rationalité*. Paris: Editions de Seuil.

Vandermeersch, Leon. 1989. "The Origin of Milfoil Divination and the Primitive Form of the *I Ching*." *Hexagrammes* 4: 5–24.

Waley, Arthur. 1958. *The Way and Its Power: A Study of the Tao Tê Ching and Its Place in Chinese Thought*. New York: Grove Press.

Wheelwright, P. 1959. *Heraclitus*. Princeton, NJ: Princeton University Press.

Wilhelm, Hellmut. 1967. "The Interplay of Image and Concept in the *Book of Changes*." *Eranos* 36: 31–57.

Wilhelm, Hellmut. 1972. "Sacrifice in the *I Ching*." *Spring* 32.

Wilhelm, Richard. 1967. "Preface." *The I Ching or Book of Changes*. Cary F. Baynes, trans. Princeton, NJ: Princeton University Press.

Yeats, William Butler. *Collected Poems*. London: Macmillan, 1952.

Yi Ching. (rpt. 1966). From *Harvard-Yenching Institute Sinological Index Series, Supplement 10: A Concordance to the Yi Ching*. Taipei: Chinese Materials and Research Aids Service Center.

3

Ethical Instinct

ROBERT BOSNAK

Ethical sense is based on instinct, as are greed, hunger, power, and sex. Just as hunger is felt as a craving for food, and greed as a craving for money, so ethics, too, is felt as a visceral abhorrence. Our societal moral system is built on our ability to feel abhorrence.

It may seem strange to ground the ethical instinct on something as lowly as the visceral sense of loathing that overtakes us when we confront what we abhor. It would seem more appealing to base ethics on a higher, more noble principle, like a craving for justice. But a longing for justice is not as deeply buried in the depth of our physical being as is disgust for things loathsome. Many of the first rules we learn in life are about what is forbidden. We are scolded, "If you do that, you are bad." In this way we learn to put reins on ourselves and to limit our gratification. Without such rules, society and culture could not exist.

Is our inculcation of values pure conditioning, like a dog's learning through punishment and reward, or do humans possess a deeper sense that enables our distinction between good and bad behavior?

We have learned from medicine that our bodies are very well able to distinguish elements which belong to them and elements which do not belong. The body goes into convulsive revulsion against foreign elements, fiercely rejecting them. Thus, there is a deep visceral distinction in the body between what is self and what is foreign. We instinctively reject the foreign. Xenophobia lives in the very cells of our body. On this innate xenophobia, society bases its capacity to teach the difference between good and bad: these acts belong, but those acts are alien. Good people act this way; our enemies act another way. We learn to growl at our enemies, to smile at our friends, and to repress actions which our society despises.

We can develop sensitivity to our ethical instincts by facing actions we despise and experience as alien, and by feeling our physical sense of revulsion toward them.

From childhood, we are instructed in the identity of our enemies. We learn to focus our abhorrence on them. We come to think of all that is despicable as the acts of our enemies.

Therefore, to become aware of what we have learned to abhor, we have to study the way we look at our enemies. In this way, we become aware of those elements of self we have been despising. Those traits we despise in our enemies are part of ourselves as well. Awareness of this makes us more fully human.

There is a limit where integration of the foreign elements is not possible because they are too repulsive. Acts can be so repulsive as to be intolerable. At this limit, we learn to differentiate between what we must learn to live with and what is to be resisted, what must be accepted as self and what is truly alien to us. At this line we learn to recognize the difference between traits we must learn to accept as human, and acts we have to resist as inhuman.

By far the majority of acts are not so extreme as to take us to the borderland between human and inhuman. But we have to know this borderland so we can recognize the difference between behavior that is acceptable and that which is not. We learn to feel viscerally more and more shades of what we can accept and what we cannot, thereby learning to trust our feelings in judgment of what is morally right and wrong action. This differentiated capacity of conscience to make its own judgments is emancipated and vastly different from the beliefs held in our social circles.

One effective way of learning about our consciences is through work on dream material. Dreams are full of terrifying actions by frightening forces. I have witnessed countless cases of people—everywhere I've done dreamwork—keeping frightening creatures out by some means or other. Keeping self safe sometimes becomes an obsession. We want to keep out what doesn't please us, those forces of the inner world whose interests oppose our carefully maintained self-images. Our desires to keep our identities intact make us resistant to everything in the inner and outer world we cannot deal with. But as long as we keep out all forces that are foreign, we can never find those elements of ourselves and the world we have to learn to live with in some form of accommodation, and those we have to battle.

In work on dreams we learn to deal with what we could not deal with and to resist what is intolerable. Therefore, the first step is letting frightening forces enter so we become aware of them.

Dream of a woman:
I'm in a square where I'll meet a monster. With me is an autistic neighbor girl. A tribunal is awaiting me. Then I confront the monster. I have terrible fears.

Scream. I am very lonely but somehow make it. At the end I am touched by a hand. First it is tender, then claws grow out of the nails. They leave deep and painful traces in my flesh. People watch me from the windows of the houses and gather around the square. Finally a man comes out who has looked on from behind one of the windows. He says:

"Yes, the emancipation of woman is connected to much suffering. Now one should not go further, it can't all be solved at once."

I am exhausted.

The central work on the dream is to re-experience the moment when the dreamer was entered by the terrifying claw. By feeling the pain again as it felt in the dream when the claw went through the skin, the dreamer can re-experience the moment when the outside world enters and the fear of the stranger all but strangles self. Let me give an example of the way this can be done through dreamwork.

I begin by asking the dreamer for a description of the square where the judgment by the tribunal takes place. The confrontation with the monster is such a frightening moment that the dreamer couldn't hold on to it; she forgot. We have to build the image up slowly so the dreamer doesn't immediately resist further exploration.

"Can you describe the square?"

"It is lined with houses. Seventeenth-century Europe. Like those places where they did executions."

"Frightening?"

"A little."

"Can you see any details?"

"I see houses. Blue, mainly. Darkish grey blue. Some houses are protruding over the street in a medieval sense. The man in the end of the dream is standing in one of the overhanging windows. The square isn't very large. There are maybe thirty people around. Anna is with me."

"Who is Anna?" (We have talked about Anna before but I want her to tell me again to get a sense of the dream figure at this moment.)

"Well, you know that she's my neighbor girl. She is completely autistic. Doesn't communicate with anyone. But lately I've been having some kind of contact with her. She sits in my kitchen when I do my chores. She likes to be with me. Sometimes she's following me around. We don't talk, but we communicate somehow."

"What is she like in the dream?"

"She's wearing summer clothes. It is a summer's eve. Light clothes. She isn't scared. I'm very scared."

"What does the fear feel like in your body?"

"It strangles me. It's apprehension. I know that something dreadful is about to happen." She shivers.

"Cold?"

She nods. "I'm scared for my life. And then I remember nothing. Just that it is horrible."

"Can you feel the horror?"

"No, I can't remember that part at all. Nothing. Like my car accident. I don't remember what happened. I have total amnesia. That's what it's like in the dream."

"Do you remember the monster?"

"He was very big. I seem to remember a bull's head. But I'm not sure. I just remember the hand. A soft hand. Very gentle."

"Where does he touch you?"

"My upper arm. On the right. He puts his hand on my bare skin. It feels pleasant."

"Can you stay with that for a moment?"

She waits a moment, feeling once again the gentle touch.

"My skin feels very soft under his hand. He seems to love me. Or at least he's very kind."

Here we have a chance to change perspective in the dream. This is a very important moment, because it is possible to feel the whole experience from another perspective than that of the habitual self. If it were possible to feel what is going on inside the monster, we have expanded the experience of the dream qualitatively. That the direct experience of the inner life of other dream figures is possible at all is based on the peculiar fact that at the basis of dream reality there lies a paradox: each figure in the dream is an element of self, and at the same time each figure in the dream is entirely independent, a self of its own. This becomes immediately apparent when we remember the way the dream was actually dreamt. In the dream there is an actual monster who behaves entirely on his own judgment, entirely independently. While dreaming, the world around us is absolutely real; that's why during dreams we are usually not aware of the fact that we are dreaming. Other presences in the dream, be they humans, animals, or even things, have their own intentions, volitions, and emotional experiences. For all we know in dream time, they are independent beings.

But from the point of view of waking consciousness, the dream appears as a representation of the personality, as the interaction of the substructures of a single personality. From this point of view, the monster is the repressed monstrosity which the dreamer has tried to keep far away from her consciousness to preserve a positive self-image. This paradox is one of the great mysteries in dreamwork, though at the same time it offers great possibilities. By empathetically feeling what the monster is feeling, we discover parts of ourselves hitherto unknown, feelings that have been hidden. At the same time, we direct daytime focus to the dream world, thereby transforming its denizens. Not only do I change, the monster changes as well.

"When his hand touches your arm, is it a light touch?"

"Yes, it is almost weightless."

"Can you feel that weightlessness?"

"It makes me float. But it is steady at the same time. His hand feels steady.

Purposeful. I can feel his sense of purpose. He wants to calm me. He doesn't want to hurt me. He just has to do something to me. Not to hurt me. He wants to get through to me. I can feel it. I can feel his desire to get through to me." She's talking very rapidly now.

"What does he want to get through to you?"

"Just that he wants to be close. I can't let my husband be close. I've never been able to let a man come close. I'm afraid of losing myself."

"And what happens when the nails grow?"

"He's getting impatient with me. He wants to get it over with. He is cruel. I can feel it now. He is cruel and dispassionate at the same time. He is cruel."

"Do you know that cruelty?"

"It's like when I tell my husband how it is. That I can't stand him around. That he bothers me. It's the truth, but I enjoy telling him and seeing him cringe."

"So the monster is trying to hurt you after all?"

"No, not really. He just likes making me see things as they are. To see reality. To destroy my rose-colored glasses. And he enjoys my discomfort. He knows how painful it is for me to face the reality of my marriage. I'd rather dream about it being a whole lot better than it is. But he won't let me."

"Can you let yourself feel his cruelty?"

"It is a shameless delight in ripping through appearances. Unmasking people. It's obnoxious. I'm obnoxious when I'm like that."

The monster is the faculty that makes the dreamer see the world around her as shamelessly real, as no prettier than it actually is. As long as the monster is kept out, she is isolated with a romanticized view of life, and at the same time she is sometimes very obnoxious to others. The cruelty of the monster is necessary for her to become conscious. In her previous condition, this capacity for consciousness was split into a virginal innocence and an occasional obnoxiousness. Bringing these inner forces together is the first step toward emancipation: becoming aware of crude life-as-it-is. A loss of innocence takes place. A painful intimacy has come into being. Intimate knowledge of her monster-side makes the dreamer cruelly aware of who she is: not pure and inviolate, but painfully aware of her own darkness. Now the dreamer can begin to see human nature as it is, not as she'd like it to be. A more realistic judgment of reality becomes possible.

The second stage in the development of an independent ethical judgment is exemplified by a man's dream experience:

I am in my home. Suddenly there is a knock on my door. It is night outside. Some disgusting slimy fellow is pushing against my door. He almost oozes through the cracks. I try to barricade the door. But I can't. Then he is inside. He smells horribly. I almost puke. He grins, knowing that he's going to get me. I wake up in terror.

While listening to the dream I was drawn to a memory of my own. Once someone was referred to me for analysis. After our first session she dreamed that, to her utter disgust, she had to drink a cup full of the spit-up of epileptics. She did not come to the next session and terminated therapy. The material that would be in the cup of analysis was too disgusting to integrate. It was too noxious.

So absorbed was I in this memory that I missed most of the dream, and I praised my good fortune over the fact I always listen to dreams twice, just for these kinds of occasions when my associations begin to reverberate off the dream. My body remembered the physical sense of revulsion I felt when I heard the spit-up dream first.

> "What do you feel in your body when you wake up?" I ask.
> "I'm nauseous," he replies, looking ready to be sick.
> "Right now?" I now notice that he is more pale than usual.
> He nods.
> "Does it have to do with the dream?" I ask carefully, not wanting to jump to conclusions.
> "I didn't feel it before. It came up when I went into the dream that second time. Then I could really feel my disgust for that slime. He is disgusting. He is like snot. He's repulsive. He's like what I felt in my lungs when I had pneumonia. That green mucus. He's sick! He makes me sick."

The slimy fellow is compared to an illness. Here is a sign that this character may be harmful. One cannot be hospitable to all forces. Some are exclusively alien and destructive. These forces have since time immemorial been called demonic.

Again I want to try and feel the situation from within the opponent of the dream-ego, to expand the emotional range of experience.

> "When you see him ooze through the door, what is it precisely that you notice?"
> "It is coming right through the cracks. Pushing its way through."
> "So there is a lot of push."
> "Yes, he's pushing very hard to get through."
> "Can you feel that push?"
> "He wants to come in very badly."
> "Why?"
> "He wants to suck me dry like a spider sucks a fly."
> "Can you let yourself feel this desire to suck someone dry?"
> There is a moment of silence. Then his face contorts.
> "What is it?"
> "It's like what I felt when my father disinherited my brother. It was such an ugly feeling, like sucking out my brother. I hated myself for it. I felt disgusting. I can still feel it when I meet my nephew after my brother died."
> I suddenly sense a moral conflict: he feels despicable about himself.
> "Just before the dream, my sister-in-law asked me to help pay for my nephew's education. I said I'd think about it. But I had already there and then made up my mind that I was going to say that I couldn't help them financially." He looks

disgusted with himself. His nausea is symptomatic for the ethical sense he has of himself at this very moment.

We are silent.

According to the laws of society this dreamer does not have obligations to his nephew. That his father disinherited his brother was not his fault, nor was his nephew's education his responsibility. But his conscience made him feel like slime. His body told him he was disgusted with himself.

The difference between the first and the second example is that in the first, the dark force has to be accepted and integrated in the self, whereas in the second dream, the slime is a disease to be repelled. The woman has to overcome her fear of the monster and becomes intimate with him, but the man has to realize his visceral revulsion against his own slimy behavior and consider going against his natural inclination to suck his brother dry.

Nature is amoral and so is natural man. But a man of conscience is able to feel sick of his own natural actions and to muster an instinctive response against greed and self-interest that is strong enough to come to a moral decision. Only our instinctive sense of ethics is strong enough to overrule our immediate self-interest. The second dreamer's instinctive greed would rather buy a new car than pay for his nephew's education. But his ability to physically feel disgusted with himself gives him pause, a moment of reflection, a moment of ethical awareness.

Is dreamwork helpful to develop a more acute sense of conscience? An ancient technique, dating back to the classical period of Greece, is called dream-incubation. The sufferer of an illness would go to the temple of the God of medicine Asclepius, in Epidaurus, to sleep in the temple precincts and wake up with a dream that would then be investigated by the priests for diagnosis and treatment. This prescribed the path toward healing.

This technique of dream-incubation can be used for any issue that feels profoundly problematic, be it one's desire to have a child and the inability to have one, an actual disease, or deep shame about some moral problem.

You take a vignette, particularly painful in its poignancy, that is a potent representation of the trouble you are in. For example: a 28-year-old man living in his widowed mother's home is engaged in a horrible fight with her, but unable to move out because he has been laid off his job. He wants to incubate a dream about the conflict with his mother. He chooses the following vignette as a most characteristic moment for everything he despises about his mother. It is a scene from the previous week: "I was out with friends and I came home at around 2:00 A.M. When I came home my mother was crying, waiting up for me. She was so damn needy. I just wanted to go to bed, but she caught me with her tears. So I sat with her for almost an hour. I hated every minute of it."

To concentrate this vignette into an incubation stimulus, it is essential that the memory is filled once more with concentrated emotionality. The easiest way to go about this is to remember as many details as possible: the quality of the light in the room at 2:00 A.M., how his body feels as he walks through the door (a little drunk), what his mother is wearing (a pink nightgown, sensuous), what it smells like in the room, the sound of his mother's sobs, how far away from her he sits, the quality of her voice as she speaks, the mounting of his irritation, feeling the bind between staying downstairs with her or going up to his room over the garage, feeling his desire to leave the house altogether, feeling the frustration about his inability to do so.

This whole exercise takes no more than five minutes just before he goes to sleep. He dreams:

I am living in an apartment. I'm putting a body through a food waste disposal. I push it down with my bare hands, unconcerned of the danger that the food disposal might cut off my hands. It gives me an elated feeling. Then I run downstairs and take the mushy leftover of the body out of a sewer pipe and put it in a garbage bag. I take the bag to the dump on my back. It is nearby. Then, as I walk the bag is getting heavier and heavier until I am almost crushed. The weight wakes me up, gasping for air. I can hardly breathe.

Our first response, of course, is that this dream portrays the anger with his mother and his desire to chop her to a pulp. However, this is hardly new information, so we try to work on the dream without preconceptions. The most productive attitude in the work with dreams is "I have no idea! I really don't know what this is all about." It is an unpleasant and disorienting feeling, but one that opens us to up the dream itself as a reality beyond our conceptual presuppositions.

"The kitchen has a lot of stainless steel. The counter is stainless, it seems as if everything is stainless. It is not a warm kitchen."

"Can you feel the atmosphere?"

"It is cold. Impersonal. Institutional. It is almost as if I'm working there. Like a cook in a restaurant. The more I look at it, the more it looks like a restaurant kitchen. I see knives hanging from the wall, glasses from the ceiling like in a bar. Pots and pans everywhere. A lot of cooking is done in this kitchen." (It seems that we are dealing with an area of the psyche where a lot of material is being processed.)

"At what point do you see the body?"

"Right from the beginning. I have my sleeves rolled up and my arms are full of blood. I keep pushing down the food waste disposal."

"What is the disposer like?"

"It's round. Only a few inches in diameter. So I don't know how I got her in there."

"Her?"

"I don't really know. I just assumed."

"Is the body dressed?"

"No. But I can't really see if it is a man or a woman. All I am really aware of is my hands."

"What do your hands feel?"

"I can feel my nails digging into the flesh."

"What is that like?" I ask, feeling repulsed.

"I just want to get rid of the body. I don't know if I have murdered her. I just know I want to get rid of it."

"Can you concentrate on that."

"I want to get rid of the body. I want to press it down. I don't want to have anything to do with it. Just want it to go away."

"What do you feel in your body?"

"My arms pushing down, especially my upper arms."

We stay silent for a while, feeling the sense of the upper arms. I'm fully concentrated on my biceps. It is very tense.

"It's like I don't want something to be. It's like I don't want to be. I sometimes feel I don't want to exist. Like when I just sit in my room over the garage, depressed, almost suicidal." His body slumps; tension is released.

"What does it feel like to carry that heavy bag?"

"I can't walk anymore. I'm pushed down. It's not as strong now as in the dream. In the dream it was exhausting and somehow humiliating. I know that feeling. It's when I can't get out of the house and just lie on my bed smoking cigarettes."

"What did you feel in the incubation memory just before you got home at 2:00 A.M.," I ask, to connect the incubation with the dream.

"I hated coming home, I just wanted to go back to the bar and drink myself to death. You know, I was glad to see my mother there. Glad that I would have to sit with her so I could get furious again about her helplessness. I like it much better to be angry with her than to be so damn depressed."

Here we have come to an ethical realization. He realizes that he is using his anger with his mother to avoid dealing with the depression. To avoid feeling that life has beaten him to a pulp, that he'd rather be dead. The ethical insight is that it is important to focus the attention on his own suicidal incapacitating depression and away from his constant bickering with his mother. Even though it seems to be *her* helplessness which is making him furious, it is his own helplessness that needs to be addressed. He can deal with his own lows even less than with his mother's tears. They're in the depression together and he can repress—push down, dispose of—his own feeling of hopelessness by focusing on hers.

Dream incubation is sometimes effective in dealing with ethical issues. It has to be remembered, however, that often there are no dreams after an incubation, or we can't find any link between the incubated problem and the dream. But it works sometimes, as in the case mentioned above, and then it can be very helpful.

Can ethical instinct be trained? The notion of instinct refers to the innate characteristics of living beings. Instinctive responses to our environment occur without conscious reflection; in their raw form they are unconscious patterns of behavior. This does not mean, however, that instincts cannot be trained into highly conscious ways of action. Let us take as an example the human instinct to communicate. If we did not have this instinct, survival would not be possible. From our earliest childhood we have to communicate in order to make our needs known. If we were not instinctively capable of relaying our distress to others, we might starve. Even something as differentiated and conscious as language is built on the basis of this instinctive urge to communicate. An instinctive urge can be refined to the equivalent of poetry. The refinement of an instinct is an art. It often leads to symbolization. The way this process comes about is described below.

The essential nature of instinct is that it is physically encoded. Its first manifestations are felt as physical sensations. Hunger is first felt as a physical pang in the stomach, and only much later in the evolution of consciousness does it lead to the culinary arts. The instinctive urge toward accumulation of matter is felt first as an immediate craving for things; it is much later that the science of economy and the craft of banking develop as differentiations of this instinctive human desire. Procreation and the accompanying urge to reproduce exist long before the development of the perfumers' art and the multi-billion-dollar cosmetics industry. One of the most important instincts of all is that of the imagination. In its raw form it creates dreams; is its refined state it creates the future.

I believe that all major human endeavors are differentiated manifestations of basic instincts. We first experience instinctive processes as physical sensations. Our education does not teach us to be aware of the intelligence of our physical being. The direct experience of our subtle physical responses to our environment is not taught in institutions of learning. This is why we live under the illusion that our instinctive urge to accumulate is ontologically different from the drive that shapes our banking system, or that ethical action is fundamentally different from instinctive revulsion toward what we abhor.

On the lowest instinctive level, what is part of us is viscerally experienced as good, and what is not part of us is experienced as bad. From the highest level of ethical instinct stems the judgment that what is humane is good and what is inhumane is bad. I believe that the same physical responses are felt on the base level of instinctual development as on the higher levels. A fundamental difference is that on a base level of instinct, these physical sensations are experienced unconsciously and lead automatically to action, while on a higher developed level of instinct, these sensations are experienced consciously and consequent actions are more or less voluntary. On a base level, there is no freedom in relation to the instinct, whereas on a higher level of consciousness there is a certain margin of independence from the instinctive pattern. Base instinct functions through an immediate sequence of stimulus and reflex; refined instinct functions filtered through the act of *reflection* between the physical stimulus and the automatic reflex.

Let us take a sideward glance at this ability to reflect, which is also a development from an innate instinctual pattern. Our capacity for reflection, our ability to insert a moment of consciousness between stimulus and response, is a differentiation of the instinct of imagination.

From birth, consciousness alternates between waking and sleeping. Much of our sleeping consciousness is spent in the dream mode. The dream mode is an innate pattern of behavior—and thus an instinct—that creates a non-physical form of reality while at the same time inhibiting responses on the physical plane. Other mammals dream as well. My dog, for example, begins to yelp in the middle of her sleep, and her paws make gestures of running. Her legs do not actually run. We can see how physical movement is inhibited as she is running in the non-physical realm of her dream world. At the moment of her dreaming, her running through the fields seems entirely real to her.

Thus, the two functions in imagination-as-instinct are: (1) the creation of a world that is experienced as entirely real but which does not exist on the physical plane, and (2) the ability to imagine possible actions without taking action on the physical plane. On the basis of these two innate functions of mammal behavior, we have developed our capacities to create and experience fiction as reality and to react to real stimuli without responding physically. The creation and experience of fiction has led to the birth of drama, film, and other arts. Our capacity to inhibit physical response to real and imagined stimuli lies at the root of our ability to reflect.

The ability to create art is an obvious benefit of the differentiation of the instinct to imagine. The value of the inhibition of physical responses to real stimuli may seem less apparent. Without this latter capacity, however, we would only have two options toward stimulation: action or repression. Both responses are problematic. Immediate instinctual response to stimuli often leads to unwanted behavior. This becomes immediately clear when we think of aggressive or sexual stimulation. Acting on these stimuli can give rise to very destructive behavior. On the other hand, repression of instinctive responses is dangerous also.

If we repress anger-responses on a regular basis, we build up a reservoir of unconscious anger that can be experienced in projection. Projection is seeing in others psychological realities we don't want to see in ourselves. Thus, repressed anger (our own anger we hide from ourselves) is experienced as the anger of others toward us. This can create an intimidated attitude because of the feeling that the whole world is angry with us. Another example is found in the dream of the man who did the incubation; by repressing his feelings of depression, he sees all depressed behavior as his mother's. By justifying his anger with her, he is unable to change his own situation.

We maneuver between these two poles of acting on instincts and repressing instincts by consciously experiencing our instinctive responses while inhibiting their enactment, much in the same way my dog instinctively inhibits the physical running action resulting from her dream.

Many people express the fear that if they let themselves experience the reality of their instinctive urges, these urges would become so strong that they would have to act on them. "Don't feed these unwanted urges," I have heard people say. In fact, the contrary is true. *The more we let ourselves experience the instinctive world in the most real fashion, the more we automatically inhibit our actions.*

The first step in the training of ethical instinct is therefore to feel our physical responses to environmental stimuli in detail, without the fear that this deeper experience of all our urges will make it more likely that we will act on them. For many people this is difficult because of their inexperience in feeling the subtle body sensations by which their somatic selves express intelligence. In my own case, this became very dramatic at the age of 20 when a profound ethical conflict led me into a deep crisis.

The values of my family had brought me to law school, where I wrestled with a life that did not suit my emotional self. I suffered from constant physical symptoms that no one was able to interpret as my organic rejection of the path I was following. My body was rejecting my life, and I did not understand my somatic responses; neither did the doctors who treated me for a host of abstruse diagnoses. Academically, I was part of the university, while my somatic intelligence had not yet entered kindergarten. I could not read my symptoms, even though they spoke in a clearer language than law books.

My moment of ethical crisis came when I had to make a decision between harming my life or the life of someone else. If I were to decide in one direction, I felt that my life would become exceedingly problematic, if not ruined. If I were to decide another way, a friend would suffer severely. Without much ethical consideration, I chose for myself. A short time after this choice, my symptoms increased to the point that I almost died, and I had to spend the better part of a year in the hospital. Without the benefit of guidance my symptoms were entirely opaque to me.

Finally, my symptoms led me into analysis, which became a prelude for my training to become an analyst myself. The ethical conflict changed the course of my life. During analysis I became aware of the fact that my body was cringing with the knowledge that in the life of my friend I had become a devil. All the muscles along the front of my stomach were in spasms, resulting in gastric problems that no doctor had been able to diagnose. Chills went through me whenever I became suddenly aware of what I had done. The shame pushed my head over to the right as if I were being attacked from the left. This put a constant pressure on my spine, which led to back troubles. I felt deep revulsion for my actions, a shame that I could not digest. Gastroenterological problems were the immediate result. My physically felt shame made me want to disappear; now I realized why I almost died; I wanted to be dead. This revulsion for my action was my first moment of profound ethical awareness. It was physically felt. Analysis made it possible for me to feel my revulsion without having to repress it in the way which had created my somatic problems. As a result, like the woman in the dream of the confrontation with the monster, I lost my innocence. I became aware of my monstrosity, without the active need to destroy myself. At the same time, it created a physical benchmark for ethical conduct. I became aware of a syndrome of physical symptoms that indicated transgression of the boundaries of ethical behavior.

Some simple exercises may clarify this connection. For example, think back to the moment in your life when you acted most unethically. Stay with this event in the same way as in the dream incubation above. Remember every detail as precisely as possible. While you do this, notice every sensation you are able to feel in your body. Concentrate on each individual phenomenon, focus on it, and hold it in your consciousness as long as possible. This exercise is very unpleasant. It confronts you with the most despicable part of yourself. It is that part which is sometimes called "shadow."

This exercise gives us a benchmark with which to compare other ethical dilemmas. By becoming aware of the physical sensations that accompany unethical action, one can begin to recognize the symptoms of unethical behavior in minor cases as well as more gross unethical actions which are usually easier to detect. Our physiological responses to unethical behavior have often been called "pangs of conscience." They are very specific for each individual, experienced differently by each person according to personal temperament and character.

The next exercise serves in the case of an ethical dilemma. Begin with the previous "benchmark" exercise, feeling the physical pangs of conscience. Now imagine all the possible outcomes of the decision. While doing this be aware of your somatic responses to the situations resulting from your decision.

For example: A married man in my analytical practice has an affair with another woman. His ethical dilemma is: should he tell his wife, continue the affair in secret, or break off with his lover?

Different sets of morals would answer this question in different ways. The Judeo-Christian set of moral values would have it that he break off the affair immediately. A culture where it is not unusual that people have affairs might say that he should continue discreetly, not telling his wife. Neither of these societal prescriptions would lead him to find his own ethical judgment in the matter.

Here follows an excerpt of an analytical session with this man.

"Whenever I think of telling Margaret (his wife), I get this terrible headache," he tells me.

"Can you tell me about the headache?" I ask.

"It begins just below my neck. The tension increases and the top of my head goes numb. Then I have this splitting headache. It comes up every time I imagine the pain in her eyes when I tell her about Helen (his lover)."

"What if you would stop seeing Helen?"

"I can't. There is no way that I can leave her. No way. That is the only thing I know for sure."

"So tell Margaret," I say provocatively.

"That's the point. When I think about telling Margaret, I get this horrific headache."

"When have you had this headache before?"

"I don't get it often."

"When was the first time you remember?"

"When I was a kid," he replies after a long pause. "I was in a boat, fishing with my little sister. My sister was about five, so I must have been around twelve. We had this little rowboat. My sister had a doll she took with her wherever she went. I still can see it very vividly. The doll was in her arms. She was sleeping. I wanted to play a joke on her, so I carefully took the doll and put it behind her on the bow of the boat. When she woke up she looked for it. She saw it sitting on the front of the boat. She grabbed for it, and the doll fell into the water and disappeared right away. She screamed. I tried to fish it out, but I couldn't find it. I felt terrible. That's when I first had that headache." Here we have the benchmark experience of unethical behavior, the physical pangs of conscience about his pleasure in torturing his kid sister.

"Please imagine telling Margaret about Helen," I suggest. "Where do you imagine telling her?"

He closes his eyes and begins to describe how he visualizes the confrontation: "I imagine it to take place in the kitchen. I'm surprised that I have such a clear image. It is definitely in the kitchen. She is cleaning up. I feel that telling her will give me a great sense of relief, even though it is very unpleasant, to say the least. But all that secrecy makes me feel terrible. So then I tell her. I can see the pain in her eyes. Now I get the headache. It has to do with the pain in her eyes."

"What does the pain look like?"

"I have destroyed her world. I have hurt her so bad. And the reason I tell her is only to get relief for myself."

"So in fact you try to rid yourself of your guilt feelings."

"Yes. I just dump it on her to feel less guilty. But when I do that I hurt her. I can feel the headache now."

"Concentrate on the headache."

I can see his forehead wrinkle as he is obviously in pain. Then he suddenly exclaims: "I shouldn't tell Margaret unless I'm willing to break up with Helen. I would only tell her to feel better myself. I shouldn't tell Margaret!"

A moment of direction has been found in this ethical dilemma between the honesty in his marriage and the pain he would inflict on his wife. The consciousness was in the headache. Inside the headache he could feel his ethical direction. Telling his wife would be unethical, since he was not willing to leave his lover, and the honesty would only serve him, not Margaret, his wife. The essential part of this example is in the fact that ethical consciousness was located in a physical symptom. An increased ability to read our physical symptoms of conscience can give us direction on the difficult road toward ethical behavior.

Like any instinct, the instinct for ethics can suffer from disorders. The hunger instinct can lead to eating disorders, greed to compulsive and ruthless exploitation, sexuality to ugly perversions; our instinct for communication can be impaired through autism, and the lust for power can become inhumane cruelty.

In the first place, our ethical instinct can be diseased. This is the case in the psychiatric disorder called psychopathy (also sometimes called sociopathy). A psychopath lacks the ability to have pangs of conscience. Sociopaths are constitutionally incapable to feel remorse, guilt, or shame about their own behavior. They can commit the most heinous crimes without blinking an eye for reasons that seem at first glance beyond the comprehension of non-psychopathic individuals. The best portrayal of a psychopath is the character of psychiatrist Hannibal Lecter, better known as Hannibal the Cannibal, played in the movie "The Silence of the Lambs." (Anthony Hopkins received the 1991 Academy Award [Oscar] for his dazzling performance.) Hannibal the Cannibal kills his victims and eats parts of them, in a rather disinterested and almost curious fashion. His total lack of attachment to his actions is a hallmark of psychopathy. Obviously, such a person, incapable of feeling remorse and so totally detached from his revolting actions, cannot develop a true sense of ethics. At best he can mimic ethics, but he cannot viscerally feel them. With this character in "The Silence of the Lambs," matters are clear. But the fact that millions of people are fascinated with this character indicates that we recognize a reality in him that lives inside all of us. We all have realms of behavior where our ethical instincts seem to have been anesthetized, where we behave detachedly in revolting ways, unable to feel shame or pangs of conscience. We need to learn about those psychopathic elements in our being. Our best sources for this information are from our enemies and partners. They know very well where these ethical weak spots lie. In these areas of behavior, we had better hold on to collective moral values, since our individual sense of ethics is lacking.

As far as ethical instinct is concerned, the opposite of psychopathy is depression. In a state of depression we constantly feel pangs of guilt about our behavior. It is impossible to differentiate between true guilt (guilt stemming from an actual ethical conflict) and depressed guilty feelings. In full-blown clinical depression, most guilt feelings stem from the depressed desire for punishment and few from actual ethical misbehavior. In the more usual cases of depressed moods, it becomes very hard to distinguish depressed guilt from pangs of conscience. Often they overlap, and instances where one would have felt only slight senses of physical discomfort are exaggerated.

An old man suffering from mood swings came to me for analysis. When he was down, he felt that he had done everything in his life wrong, especially the way he had treated his children. He felt horrible about the way he had dealt with them while they were growing up. When he was on the upswing, he did not feel any remorse about his child rearing. It became clear during analysis that he had been quite a deficient father, though there had been many extenuating circumstances. Neither the ethical judgment in his downswing that he was despicable, nor the carefree attitude of his upswing was adequate. For a while, it was my task to remind him of the mood at the opposite end of the swing in relation to his children. Over the course of therapy, he developed a more realistic attitude in relation to his children, and he was able to regain a sense of ethical judgment toward them. He no longer acted toward them either through guilty humiliation or carefree neglect. He was able to feel that he had done things wrong in the past, and to be sad about it, without dropping down into feelings of exaggerated self-recrimination.

At this point it is important to insert a word of warning about modern forms of Western psychotherapy. Many therapists feel that all guilt is wrong, or that people should express themselves free of guilt. When I hear this, I feel blood rushing to my head and rage surging up from my belly. These somatic symptoms show me that I feel this psychotherapeutic attitude to be revolting, and therefore I judge it unethical. This "therapeutic" attitude creates monstrous, infantile individuals who are sick with entitlement and incapable of an ethical sense, because their instinctive ethics are systematically ruined by their therapists who encourage them to feel free of the pangs of conscience that are essential for the differentiation of individuated ethics.

This leads us to consider the second form of ethical disorder, that inflicted by society. Of course, it is not only therapists who create monsters. A youth must dull his ethical sensibility just to survive in the American inner city where drugs rule and poverty strikes deeply into the heart of broken families. This process of numbing is a loss of soul. Soul refers to the richness of our inner life, to a sense of self that is steeped in a feeling of the presence of interior forces. It is ultimately linked to a sense of identity. When drugs and violence kill the soul, there is no interior space left in which to experience the elements of which self consists, like the instincts. Then the inner sense of direction is unavailable. We need a sense of inner self to have ethical consciousness.

However, as long as there is a vestige of a sense of a self that can act in the world, a self that has not become entirely submerged into the passivity of the surrounding misery, an individual can feel pangs of conscience. This conscience may be very different from that of a person living in less dismal circumstances. For example, it may not experience killing as unethical, but other actions, like betraying friends, might produce ethical symptoms in much the same fashion as described above.

If a person is suddenly removed from such a battlefield, and some of the numbing disappears, horrifying ethical symptoms can occur, sometimes leading to suicide. These experiences have been observed both in American Vietnam veterans and in Soviet Afghan veterans. Once returned to the world outside the war, remorse expresses itself in a host of physical symptoms, from insomnia and nightmares to psychosomatic disorders and suicide. Interviews with these veterans reveal that actions committed without much hesitation or afterthought come to haunt soldiers during their nightmare battlefields long after the events. Hardened men who followed orders to kill suddenly become identified with their victims. This shows that the ethical instincts still function in these war zones, but that soldiers have been anesthetized to deal with the immediate situation. A sense of abhorrence of the actions of self and others remains. It is just not consciously experienced.

A powerful expression of ethical instinct is *outrage*. Our ability to feel outrage is one of the most valuable capacities we have. Outrage is the ethical response to intolerable situations that can lead us to passionate action. Whoever cannot feel outrage at the sins of the world has a partially numbed ethical instinct. But outrage is a raw, instinctive response. For outrage to lead to refined action and not just to a fanatical outburst of ethical passion, it must undergo training, much in the way I have described above. The great example of such training in restrained ethical outrage was given to us by Mahatma Gandhi, the liberator of India. In his autobiography, he writes a warning against embarking on expressions of ethical outrage without proper preliminary training:

A *Satyagrahi* [disciple of Gandhi's ethical system] obeys the laws of society intelligently and of his own free will, because he considers it his sacred duty to do so. It is only when a person has thus obeyed the laws of society scrupulously that he is in a position to judge as to which particular rules are good and just and which unjust and iniquitous. Only then does the right accrue to him of civil disobedience of certain laws in well defined circumstances. My error lay in my failure to observe this necessary limitation. I called on the people to launch upon civil disobedience before they had thus qualified themselves for it, and this mistake seemed to me of Himalayan magnitude.

In other words, Gandhi let the people break out in outrage and thereby created a very violent response, because the system of restraint was not in place, though the outrage was entirely justified. The fundamental principle of non-violence was discarded. Outrage has to be felt and experienced through to its final conclusion, which is usually very violent. But by first experiencing it in imagination, it can be held in check when action follows. Only in this way it is possible to act on the feeling of outrage and remain non-violent. Non-violence is important, according to Gandhi, because violence breeds violence. The restraint that results from ethical training can absorb violent impulses and transform them into symbolic action.

This became most clear when Gandhi carried out his stroke of ethical genius. He marched with thousands of followers to the beach and picked up a handful of salt. The production of salt was only allowed to the British government at the time. By holding up a handful of salt, Gandhi symbolically demonstrated his outrage through a creative act of civil disobedience that proved to be more powerful than the entire British Empire.

At this point we can observe one of the important elements of ethical action that I have not yet mentioned: *refined ethical action, because it is based on a combination of instinct and imagination, is inherently creative.* Raw ethical instinct leads to actions that are instinctively driven. They are not creative, because they have no element of imagination in them. The mixture of the two instincts, ethics and imagination, can lead to a creative transformation of the potential raw act into *gesture*. Gesture is a dramatic creative action that generates symbolization in the observer and thereby can move the observer to responses. Gandhi's ethical genius could create gesture from outrage, thereby profoundly moving the hearts of millions. A creative act of outrage is usually more potent than a literal expression.

What Gandhi calls "following the laws of society scrupulously in order to judge which ones are just and which are not," I have referred to as the training of the ethical instinct by carefully observing all the variations of somatic responses to situations we abhor. In this way we hone our responses and can trust our outrage when it comes up.

Sometimes, of course, the outrage is so great that inhibition cannot restrain it from direct action. Then something like sleepwalking takes place. The necessity of the image is felt so strongly that it breaks through the inhibition and action follows. This can be seen in ethical conflicts that have overheated, like the struggles in the Middle East. So much blood has flowed that it becomes very difficult to find ways to make outrage express itself indirectly. A creative form of symbolization has to be found. This is one reason why peace conferences spend so much time on conflicts over the shape of the table, or on other matters that seem trivial. These deliberations stem from the necessary admixture of imagination and symbolization to raw outrage, which create dramatic gesture. Under normal circumstances, if the ethical instinct is scrupulously trained, moments when the image breaks through the inhibition and becomes literal action are exceptions.

Why train our sense of ethics at all? Very often it is possible to be guided by the prescriptions of society. Much of the time, however, decisions need to be made in specific situations, often ambiguous, where collective prescriptions are no guide. Sometimes, one even has to go against collective morality to follow one's conscience.

With the world becoming increasingly complex, relationships less traditional, stereotypes under attack, and roles more vaguely defined, we increasingly have to trust our own judgments. Developing this capacity for judgment is essential in these chaotic times. It can give structure to behavior, passion to action, and guidance to moments of confusion.

As I have indicated, a trained ethical instinct often leads to action directed toward correcting elements in self and society which outrage one. It also may lead to a longing for change, and a vision of a future that is different from the status quo. This longing is not just a hope or a wish, but a visceral necessity based on the urge to correct what we abhor. There is a difference between such an urgent, somatically felt necessity and a mere wish or hope. In the former case, we are compelled to action by an inevitable drive like other instincts, whereas with hopes and wishes, an image pulls our minds, but it does not necessarily lead our bodies to inevitable action.

This ethical longing is not a fanatical outburst of utopian passion, because it has gone through a training of ethical imagination which has created sufficient inhibitions. Utopian fanaticism leads to literal acts of violence that do nothing but create more violence. As rawhides cured in lye become leather, ethical outrage that has cured sufficiently in imagination leads to creative acts that bring about new situations.

I want to conclude with my own vision of ethics, both intimately personal as well as made from universal building blocks. Based on my experience of working with people's dreams in Western Europe, the United States, Eastern Europe, Australia, and Japan, I believe that on an essential level, people are much more similar than different. Therefore, assessments which make certain peoples into monsters are based on a lack of self-knowledge. We are all capable of monstrous behavior, and we would remain in a constant state of shame if we were not "blessed" with the ability to pretend to ourselves that we are better than we, deep down, actually are. We are able to keep up this pretense as long as we can feel ourselves the victims of the monstrous behavior of others. Therefore I believe that it is essential for all of us to develop our ethical instincts. Only in that way can we deal with our own monstrosities as well as those of others, and find creative responses to our shady drives.

With a developed sense of ethics, we have to work on those societal problems we most abhor. The social problem I most abhor is that based upon xenophobia, the dread of strangers. I abhor this fundamental element of the human make-up when it is put into actions where one group of people acts superior to another. I hate this kind of behavior with a passion that is strong enough that I am willing to fight it whenever I can. In the same way, I despise myself when I display this kind of attitude in myself.

I therefore believe it to be of the essence to bring people of different backgrounds together to let them experience each other's dreams. When you feel the dream of another person in a deeply emotional fashion, it becomes impossible to feel that person to be fundamentally different from yourself. This urge became clear to me during my analysis. I had a persistent dream in which an old grandfather from Eastern Europe (historically I have no such grandfather) told me that he wanted to get to know the world and to understand the lives of different peoples through the study of their dreams. This has remained the central focus in my life.

On a larger scale, I believe it to be important that people discuss with each other their societal dreams. For example, many peoples believe that they are chosen above all others. Their dream is that they are better or more valuable than all others. This gives them a feeling of having a special destiny that makes them chosen over all other peoples. Jews have it and Japanese have it, Native American tribes have it, White Americans have it, Germans have it, and probably most others have this myth as well. This chosen feeling, this feeling of specialness, is one of the most dangerous emotions in the soul. As long as we take it literally, we believe that we are indeed the chosen people, better than anyone else. This can lead to war and destruction, as we know only too well from the Second World War. But when we are able to find out that we have a speical destiny *as humans*, something we have mistranslated into our ethnic delusions of superiority, then our privilege of having been born as human beings becomes the motivating factor to give a content to the notion of humanity, what it is to have been born human.

We are born human, but not necessarily humane. Just look at little children, and see how inhumanly they often act toward each other. Our struggle as humans is to learn that humanity has an obligation to the world, because we humans act on the world more than any other living beings. Being human means that we know that our actions matter to the world into which we were born. Being human means that our life is at the heart of an ironic paradox: on the one hand, we are insignificant accidents existing on a tiny planet circling a small star in the outskirts of one of some trillion galaxies, flying with unimaginable speed through an ever-vaster universe. On the other hand, we are unique in the comsos, as possibly the only miracle of life anywhere that has a certain amount of freedom to choose between more or less refined instinctive responses. It is this very choice to refine or not to refine our instinctive behavior that makes us different from other species. It is this choice that makes us truly human. Therefore, we have to harness the outrage we feel about the destruction of the world around us and to transform it into coherent gestures, generating a longing in people to counteract the destruction of a world in which, as humans, we are the "chosen."

A few hundred years from now, no one will remember our names, let alone our lives and actions. All our quests for immortality are futile. The only certainty that exists is that we will be forgotten. Even the most illustrious human is only remembered for a few moments of her or his existence. Actions matter not because we will be remembered for them, because we won't. Ethical actions are necessary to the soul. Our inner life would wither without them, and so would the world. As I have shown, refined ethical instinct is by necessity creative because it transforms raw outrage into refined symbolic acts, like Gandhi's Salt March. This essentially creative human capacity, to transform base instinct into creative symbol, makes each truly ethical act a continuation of raw creation that is going on constantly all around us. However, it creates something entirely new, something that has never existed before. Each ethical response is a work of art, a transformation of raw nature into refined culture, its value as self-evident as any artistic creation.

4

Synchronicity and the Transformation of the Ethical in Jungian Psychology

ROBERT AZIZ

Considerable interest is emerging today in the spiritual teachings of the aboriginal peoples of North America. The spirituality of the First Nations peoples parallels the worldview of traditional Chinese philosophy in being decidedly unitary in character. This would not have surprised the Swiss psychiatrist and founder of analytical psychology, Carl Gustav Jung (1875–1961). Jung believed that the central problem of the modern world was meaninglessness or soullessness, to put it in spiritual terms. Jung also believed that our present loss of meaning and soul largely stems from our state of spiritual disconnectedness from nature.

In his Terry Lectures on psychology and religion delivered at Yale University (1937), Jung spoke of the shift he was witnessing from an external, historically based religious experience to a natural, experientially based religious experience. A historically based religious experience in the form of a narrow and fixed system of symbols was clearly losing its value for increasing numbers of people in the West. An alternative was what Jung described as "immediate religious experience," by which he meant a direct and conscious encounter with nature—the spontaneously manifesting contents of the unconscious.[1]

Eliade tells us that the figure of the shaman whom we find in Native American and other nature-based traditions "is the great specialist in the human soul; he alone 'sees' it, for he knows its 'form' and its destiny."[2] As an illustration of the unique ability of the shaman to see what others simply cannot see, it is said that a shaman can predict a thunderstorm by looking at a perfectly blue sky. In 1937, Jung was certainly looking at a perfectly blue sky that would remain blue for several decades, well into the 1960s. Yet, like the shaman, Jung foresaw what others did not, because his vision was turned not toward the outwardly manifest, but rather toward the activities and patterns of the psyche, the soul.

The thunderstorm that was seen and predicted by Jung is now upon us. What in 1937 was largely hidden and unrecognized—a movement toward a nature-based spirituality—is now in the forefront of the experience of a vast number of people in the grip of a newly emerging, nature-based worldview. This is a worldview in which the psychological is not split off from the spiritual. It is a worldview in which evil is not simply projected "out there." It is a worldview in which people live in conscious relationships to their bodies and their sexuality. It is a worldview in which the feminine principle is respected. Most importantly, it is a unitary worldview in which God, the Tao, the Creator, or the Absolute is viewed not as over and above, but rather as present in, yet not necessarily subsumed by, all of nature. This is the nature-based worldview and spirituality of which Jung spoke in 1937. It is the worldview to which Jung believed his psychology would give special access.

The interest today in the spiritual teachings of the aboriginal peoples of this land would not have surprised Jung. Decades ago, Jung knew that the worldview coming to him through his own journey into the unconscious, as well as that which he clinically observed emerging in the psychological processes of others, resonated with the spiritual worldview of the peoples of the First Nations. Accordingly, when Marie-Louise von Franz, one of Jung's closest disciples, remarked to Jung that his spiritual orientation was at times not unlike that of the Naskapi Indians "who have neither priest nor ritual but who merely follow their dreams which they believe are sent by the 'immortal great man in the heart'," Jung answered, "Well, that's nothing to be ashamed of, it's an honor!"[3]

Within the Jungian worldview, the interface of the conscious and unconscious is the place of revelation—"immediate religious experience." Because experience of revelation is not historically fixed but ongoing and dynamic, the ethical perspective that flows out of this dialogue is equally dynamic. More specifically, we could say that ethics, rather than constituting a set law or code of behavior, relates to the unconscious. As Jung puts it in his foreword to Neumann's *Depth Psychology and a New Ethic*, the ethical relates to how one "[brings] the conscious and the unconscious into responsible relationship. We might therefore define 'new ethic' as a development and differentiation within the old ethic, confined at present to those uncommon individuals who, driven by unavoidable conflicts of duty, endeavor to bring the conscious and the unconscious into responsible relationship."[4]

The ethical problem of bringing "the conscious and unconscious into responsible relationship" can be conceived in terms of two separate problems. First, there is the problem of correctly interpreting the meaning of the exchange between the conscious and the unconscious. Second, there is the problem of grounding this meaning in the soil of one's own life.

The Jungian model regards the psyche as a self-regulating system. The process by which the psyche is regulated is termed "psychic compensation." The unconscious utilizes a vast array of symbols to address both the immediate and long-term needs of consciousness. Through its compensatory symbols, the unconscious speaks to our present day-to-day problems from a perspective which takes into account the past, present, and future developmental needs of the individual.

Our everyday experiences trigger unconscious themes of which we may not be aware. The more unaware one is of the unconscious theme in question, the more problematic it tends to be. For example, the experience of drawing romantically closer to another individual may trigger an unconscious theme constructed out of past experiences of intimacy. If that activated theme contains unpleasant memories, an alarm goes off telling the individual to pull away because intimacy is dangerous. At the conscious level, the individual then begins to rationalize why the relationship cannot work. The problem is a defect not in the present relationship, but rather in his or her experience of intimacy, projected onto the present relationship.

In situations such as this, the unconscious compensates through dream symbolism, by showing not only unconscious themes, but also their ultimate resolutions with the long-term developmental needs of the individual in mind.

The resolution of such repressed emotional themes, which Jung termed "complexes," often involves the compensatory activation of what he called "archetypes." In contrast to the personal unconscious consisting of the forgotten contents of one's life that cluster to form complexes, the archetypal or collective unconscious is common to all people. One of the truly distinguishing features of the Jungian model of the psyche is the understanding, based on the clinical observation of the process of psychic compensation, that the unconscious contains transpersonal solutions to transpersonal problems. Human beings struggle with transpersonal problems related to relationships and marriage, religious conceptions, sexuality, and death, to name but a few. Accordingly, when life confronts us with these problems, the psyche responds with transpersonal symbols paralleling the universal themes found in religious and mythological literature, although often outside of the range of the subject's personal experience and knowledge.

One example of such transpersonal compensation is the dream of a five-year-old boy. The boy's younger brother had become ill with a neurological disorder that resulted in his sudden and unexpected death. The whole family was grief-stricken, especially the children, who sought understanding as much as adults. During this time of crisis, the five-year-old dreamt that his aunt sneezed, and that the baby was now alive and well. They could go and pick him up at the hospital.

The five-year-old child certainly did not know that the reason we say "God bless you" when someone sneezes is that it has long been believed the soul may escape the body at that moment, in the absence of an appropriate blessing. The child would not have known that that belief likely came from the notion that breath and life are one and the same, such as we find in Genesis 2:7: "And the Lord God formed man of the dust of the ground, and breathed into his nostrils the breath of life; and man became a living soul."[5] Nor would the child have known that his dream was a rebirth dream in which the soul of his brother was being reborn following his death through the sneeze of his aunt, much as the soul carried within a woman for nine months is separated from her body at the moment of birth. Having been the child's caregiver when his mother was at work, his aunt was a most appropriate choice as the second mother through which the second birth should occur. The five-year-old child certainly would not have understood the subtleties of interpretation I have presented here to illustrate transpersonal compensation. What the child did know, however, was that his brother who had died was now alive.

Through the process of psychic compensation, the unconscious draws on both personal psychic experiences and rich transpersonal meanings carried within the deeper archetypal layers of the psyche, generating healing symbols to address the immediate and long-term developmental needs of the individual. In the form of the compensatory activities of the unconscious, nature is thus both purposive and progressive, and I would add, intrinsically moral. Through its compensatory activities, nature seeks nothing less than the progressive unfoldment of our conscious journey toward self-realization, that Jung termed "individuation."

If nature in the form of the unconscious is indeed intrinsically moral, and works unceasingly through its compensatory activities to bring about the self-realization of the personality, it follows that the meaning which comes to one in the process of individuation through psychic compensation must not only be correctly interpreted, but also planted in the soil of one's own life, and not simply left to perish unattended. "With the advance toward the psychological," Jung reflects, "a great change sets in, for self-knowledge has certain ethical consequences which are not just impassively recognized but demand to be carried out in practice."[6]

When the insights that come to one through the compensatory activities of nature are not "carried out in practice," the consequences to the individual can be quite serious. The most dangerous development is the erosion of one's connection to life and meaning—a loss of soul. In dreams, this experience of disconnectedness from meaning is often portrayed in representations that suggest a cheapening of the sacred. For example, an individual dreams that he is on a religious pilgrimage, but just as he is about to mount the steps of the holy place, he hesitates and turns back. At that very moment, what in the dream had been a truly religious site now turns into a carnival-like atmosphere with people everywhere selling cheap relig-ious trinkets. One often has such a dream when one has done exactly the same thing in one's life: hesitated and turned back at a critical moment when something must be carried forward in practice.

As well as the carnival-like or game-like atmosphere in these dreams, there is usually another fatal element, which the dreamers either do not sufficiently acknowledge or actually fail to comprehend altogether. What is being treated as a game is in fact not a game at all. The gun is being handled as if it contains blanks, when the ammunition is live. It is now simply a matter of time before that shocking reality breaks through into the life of the subject.

In summary, it should be emphasized that the conscious and unconscious intersect at the place of revelation, "immediate religious experience." As early as 1937, Jung spoke of the emergence of a nature-based spirituality, by which he meant a depth experience of a conscious relationship to the purposive and progressive compensatory activities of nature through the unconscious. Just as revelation in the Jungian worldview is dynamic and ongoing, so, too, is the ethical position which emerges. As we have seen, the ethical relates to the manner in which we approach the compensatory activities of the unconscious and work with them: how we bring "the con-scious and unconscious into responsible relationship." In conclusion, the ethical is the manner in which the encounter with the compensatory sym-bols of the unconscious is both held in consciousness and enacted in one's own life.

"Synchronicity" is a term coined by Jung to explain the meaningful par-alleling of internal (intrapsychic) and external events. Jung theorized that the synchronicity principle constitutes an acausal principle in nature which functions as something of a complement to the causality principle. If one were to dream of the arrival of a letter from an individual, and the next day were to receive a letter from this same individual, we would have an instance of what Jung termed synchronicity. As with other synchronistic experiences, we have in this example a meaningful paralleling of two caus-ally unrelated events: an intrapsychic event (the dream about the letter), and an external event (the arrival of the letter).

It is generally the case that the compensatory meaning of dream contents is determined by subjective level analysis. That is, the various figures and objects of the dream refer exclusively to aspects of the dreamer's own per-sonality. To illustrate this we can use our above example.

If we were to apply a subjective level interpretation to this dream, we would view the letter as a communication from one component of the dreamer's personality to another. In applying a subjective level interpreta-tion, we need to know the traits the dreamer associates with the personality of the correspondent, in order to determine what aspect of the dreamer's own personality is attempting to be heard. For the purposes of demonstration, let us say the correspondent represented someone with a more differentiated value structure than that held by the dreamer. In a subjective level interpretation, the letter in question would be regarded as a compensatory communication from this unrecognized yet much-needed aspect of the dreamer's own personality. More specifically, the unconscious would be viewed as communicating to the subject the need to develop a more differentiated value structure through the symbol of the letter.

This is what meant is meant by subjective level interpretation. As this and many similar clinical examples indicate, subjective level interpretation alone does not always do justice to the meaning of a dream. The dream informs us not only of an intrapsychic arrangement, but also of a parallel objective arrangement that takes place the following day—the arrival of the letter. In clinical examples such as this, the exclusive focus on subjective level interpretation, which has characterized Jungian psychology from its inception, falls away. This is the point where the synchronicity theory enters, with its far-reaching implications for the Jungian worldview.

The Jungian concept of nature as intrapsychic compensation is the worldview upon which we have focused much of our attention and in which the majority of Jungians continue to reside. In the synchronistic worldview, nature is understood to compensate consciousness both inwardly and outwardly, not simply intrapsychically, such as we saw with the doubling of the letter symbol in our above example. However, compensatory activities of nature are not always present or identifiable both inwardly and outwardly. Accordingly, we can think in terms of two types of synchronistic experiences: (1) where the compensatory activity of nature is identifiable both inwardly and outwardly, such as in our above example, and (2) where the compensatory activity of nature is identifiable outwardly only.

The dream about the letter, as well as the actual arrival of the letter the following day, is an expression of the same compensatory pattern: the need for the subject to develop a more differentiated value structure. With synchronistic experiences of the first type, both inner and outer manifestations of the same compensatory theme exist independently. In that the dream did not cause the letter to arrive nor vice versa, the removal of one does not invalidate the compensatory import of the other. In contrast to synchronistic experiences of the first type, where the compensatory activities of nature are experienced both inwardly and outwardly, synchronistic experiences of the second type describe experiences where external compensatory events are the only identifiable manifestations of the psychophysical patterns. In terms of our example, that would be a situation where in the absence of a dream about the letter, the arrival of the letter itself were the only identifiable manifestation of the constellated psychophysical pattern.

Just as a timely call from a friend may serve to lift the spirits of a person struggling with the isolation of having just moved to a different city, so, too, can the timely arrival of a letter alter one's psychic orientation, and thus be of equally genuine compensatory import. The compensatory "click" that takes place between the conscious orientation of the subject and the objective synchronistic event is certainly real enough when it happens. An interesting example of a synchronistic experience of this second type took place between Jung and Henry F. Fierz.

In the 1950s, Fierz was charged with the task of seeing the manuscript of a deceased scientist through to publication. The firm to which Fierz had submitted the work was not sure about its suitability for publication and instructed Fierz to get Jung's opinion. After Jung had had time to examine the manuscript, he called Fierz in to render his verdict. Jung opposed publication and refused to yield to Fierz's arguments to the contrary. The matter seemed settled when Jung looked at his watch to dismiss Fierz. Somewhat startled, Jung paused and asked Fierz: "When did you come?" To which Fierz replied: "At five, as agreed." Jung: "But that's queer. My watch came back from the watchmaker this morning after a complete revision, and now I have 5:05. But you must have been here much longer. What time do you have?" Fierz: "It's 5:35." Jung then said to Fierz, "So you have the right time and I the wrong one. Let us discuss the thing again." Fierz was then able to convince Jung to support publication.[7]

With this example of the second type of synchronistic event, we see how Jung fully received the compensatory response of nature, manifested only externally. Knowing what he did about synchronistic compensation, Jung recognized that he was in error, not Fierz. Jung recognized that the decision to oppose publication had been premature. He stopped, just as his watch had, when indeed he needed to be open to discussion.

In summary, we have seen how nature compensates consciousness both inwardly and outwardly within the synchronistic worldview. The ethical is not confined simply to that which arises out of the dialogue between the conscious and the unconscious. The ethical is the manner in which, inwardly and outwardly, the encounter with the compensatory activities of nature is both held in consciousness and enacted in one's own life.

Jung first introduced the synchronicity theory in 1928[8] in a private lecture to a group of his followers. His first public presentation took place two years later in an address in memory of the sinologist Richard Wilhelm.[9] Jung continued to refer to synchronicity in his lectures and essays, and most importantly, worked with it in his analytical practice. It was not until 1952, however, that he produced a paper which sought "to give a consistent account of everything I have to say on the subject."[10] The resulting paper, unfortunately, fell far short of its intended goal. A most curious shortcoming of this paper was Jung's failure to address adequately the clinical aspects of synchronicity.

The literature on synchronicity that has followed in the wake of Jung's principal essay has repeated the error of Jung's own work. Accordingly, the clinical application of synchronicity has remained ungrounded, and the attendant transformations of the Jungian worldview that such a grounding reveal have remained veiled. The Jungian world has an inner orientation which weakens the ethical in the analytical process itself.

In analysis, the progressive compensatory meanings of the unconscious are vulnerable to being treated merely aesthetically, sliced to accommodate the aesthetic sensitivities of the subject. As Jung writes: "We allow the images to rise up, and maybe wonder about them, but that is all. We do not take the trouble to understand them, let alone draw ethical conclusions from them."[11] Approaching analysis from such a position, the analysand tends to experience his or her process in the manner most individuals experience a good film or play. One goes to the theater, one may be deeply moved and even in tears, yet one's life remains unchanged when one leaves the theater. In analysis, such an analysand simply watches the drama unfold without experiencing himself or herself as an actual participant in the reality of the situation.

Meanings emerge differently, however, when one is confronted with the synchronistic pattern of nature "out there." No longer is one viewing things from the comfortable position of a theater chair; rather, one is right in the unfolding drama, and the need to get the compensatory message and implement the necessary changes is pressing. Synchronicity releases the individual from the quicksand-like trap of the merely aesthetic into the ethical. This is especially true of synchronistic *shadow* intrusions.

The "shadow" is a Jungian technical term used to describe the unknown and often inferior side of the personality. Jungian psychology understands masculine and feminine principles to operate within both men and women, so the shadow problem is not confined exclusively to men.

Whereas the masculine principle in Jungian psychology is associated with differentiation and goal orientation, the feminine principle is associated with inclusiveness and relatedness.[12] With respect to problems of ethics, the masculine principle is understood to process according to principles; the feminine according to situations. It is interesting to note that Carol Gilligan reached similar conclusions in her study of how decisions are reached by women on the issue of abortion. Without reference to Jung's work, Gilligan also concluded that the long-standing Freudian characterization of women as amoral stems from the fact that Freud himself failed to recognize that women simply do not process moral problems in the same manner as men do.[13]

In the Jungian framework, the masculine and feminine principles optimally function in a balanced relationship to each other, so one-sidedness in either direction is problematic. The unrelated masculine shows itself as obsessive preoccupation with principle at the expense of human feeling, or willfulness at the cost of self-relationship and relationship to others. In this sense, the unrelated masculine is like an army tank which simply runs over everything in its path to get toward its destination. The following example of synchronistic shadow intrusion involves the problem of the unrelated masculine.

The analysis of the shadow is never a painless undertaking. Indeed as one moves into shadow analysis, one often feels that one would have had second thoughts had one known the dark depths into which the work would be heading. The analysand whose case material we are now about to examine was at such a point of discouragement. The old adage "things are going to get worse before they get better" provided little comfort. The analysand, like most people, simply wanted to move away from the darkness of the masculine shadow into "more positive stuff" in his analysis, yet to do so at that time would require him to pull back prematurely on the shadow work underway. Then he would have to deal with the very problem he had not sufficiently worked through in his own analysis, a problem he had not been trained to address.

The evening of the day he recorded this very concern in his journal, he dreamt that he was working in a hospital treating patients, even though he did not have the medical training or license to do so. He was going to treat a man with a "trigger finger."

The image of the analysand going to treat a condition he had not been trained or licensed to treat reflects his dilemma. His dream was telling him that, one way or another, he was going to have to deal with the problem of the "trigger finger," a most appropriate symbol of the unrelated masculine.

"Trigger finger" is a medical condition in which a nodule on the tendon prevents it from sliding smoothly in the tendon sheath. When one goes to flex the finger, one must use greater than normal force to move it. Once the finger finally has moved, it becomes stuck in the bent position and can be freed only by being straightened by the other hand. In reference to the problem of the unrelated masculine, "trigger finger" symbolizes no middle ground, no smooth movement between inaction and action, passivity and overkill.

The above dream was followed in the next two days by further dreams dealing with the masculine shadow. In one dream, the analysand was traveling on a subway train to a destination which could only be reached through the underground, when he suddenly realized that some thugs had re-routed the train so it was about to collide with another. He got off and notified the appropriate authorities, who stopped the train just before it would have collided with one that was approaching on the same track. The next day he dreamt that he was on his way to a sporting event, driving down the road half asleep, unable to awaken. He was concerned about being stopped by the police for impaired driving.

The first dream points out that to reach his intended destination the analysand must take the subway, that is to say, move through the underground world of the unconscious. Here in this underground world, he encounters the thugs, shadow figure symbols of the unrelated masculine who are out to create a tremendous collision. Recognizing this, the analysand gets off the train and notifies the appropriate authorities before the collision takes place. In the second dream, the crisis intensifies. Indeed what is barely escaped in the first dream moves closer to disaster in the second one. Here the analysand at the wheel on his way to a sporting event is just about to be knocked unconscious by the complex.

The compensatory patterning of the theme of the unrelated masculine was certainly not limited to the intrapsychic. Several days later, the analysand attended the play "A Walk in the Woods," which proved to be of considerable compensatory import. The play unfolds around discussions of arms reduction that take place between an American diplomat and his Soviet counterpart. The American is new to the work, and consequently far more idealistic about what is taking place. On the other hand, the seasoned Soviet is more than aware of the limitations of the process. He recognizes that the "negotiations" are staged for the sake of political considerations in their own countries and abroad. He knows that the two men will not formulate real policy. He focuses his attention not so much on the "negotiations," but on the more meaningful problem of getting to know his American counterpart as a person. He does this by encouraging the American to join him for walks in a nearby park—an involvement the American initially perceives as unprofessional.

The critical event in the play takes place when the American is walking by himself on a break in Geneva. He drops a piece of paper on the ground and suddenly finds himself being berated for littering by a Swiss policeman. The American's idealistic sense of his own self-importance, which has already suffered several blows, reaches its limits of tolerance. His diplomatic persona shatters, and the unrelated masculine seizes control. He pushes the policeman and flashes his diplomatic card to a gathering crowd in a frenzied and desperate struggle to convince them of his importance. Recalling the incident to the Soviet, who joins him in the park for their walk, the American later experiences shock and dismay at his own behavior.

This breaking through of the diplomat's unrelated masculine side from behind the persona of political idealism brings into the foreground the real problem of the arms race, that is, the problem of the shadow. Jung always maintained that our only way out of this dilemma is psychological wholeness, not idealism. With striking relevance to this issue, in a work completed only ten days before his death, Jung wrote:

If, for a moment, we regard mankind as one individual, we see that the human race is like a person carried away by unconscious powers; and the human race also likes to keep certain problems tucked away in separate drawers. . . . Our world is, so to speak, dissociated like a neurotic, with the Iron Curtain marking the symbolic line of division. Western man, becoming aware of the aggressive will to power of the East, sees himself forced to take extraordinary measures of defense, at the same time as he prides himself on his virtue and good intentions.

What he fails to see is that it is his own vices, which he has covered up by good international manners, that are thrown back in his face by the communist world, shamelessly and methodically. What the West has tolerated, but secretly and with a slight sense of shame (the diplomatic lie, systematic deception, veiled threats), comes back into the open and in full measure from the East and ties us up in neurotic knots. It is the face of his own evil shadow that grins at Western man from the other side of the Iron Curtain.[14]

For Jung, psychological wholeness and social/political action are inseparably linked, and in moving into either of these areas, we must especially come to terms with the shadow. We cannot make the world a safer and better place to live if we cannot come to terms with the shadows in our own lives. Not surprisingly, the analysand's dreams on the evening of the play returned to the problem of the unrelated masculine. In one dream, a Volkswagen Beetle, a common dream symbol of the emerging wholeness of the self, was reduced to a crumpled mass of metal after trying to pull a much larger car out of a depression in the land. In the second dream, the analysand found himself in a doughnut shop buying up all the "good ones," knowing that the "passive" man standing behind him in line would not get any of them.

The excesses of the unrelated masculine as well as their consequences both to self and others are well depicted in these dreams. The first dream, in which a smaller car is destroyed while trying to pull a much larger car out of a depression, demonstrates how one seriously injures oneself through the excess of the unrelated masculine. This is the case, for instance, when the unrelated will of one individual goes up against that of another who is even more willful, or where one simply takes on a struggle or task where defeat is certain. The second dream shows how the excess of the unrelated masculine injures or deprives others. In both dreams, the analysand is being directed away from the excess of the unrelated masculine toward an experience of balance and relatedness.

Given all that had taken place, the analysand certainly knew that he was inextricably involved in the problem of the masculine shadow. Both inwardly and outwardly, he had become engaged by the compensatory activities of nature in this problem, yet his drop into the unrelated masculine was not over.

The following day, he was driving slowly along a road looking for a parking spot. Having searched the area for a place to park, he glanced ahead and suddenly realized he was at a pedestrian crosswalk. Slamming on the brakes, he brought his car to a stop just across the pedestrian line.

He was in front of his hospital. Looking to his left, he saw a group of men coming toward him. One was yelling angrily at him for not having yielded properly. As the man approached his car window, the analysand's feelings suddenly shifted from shock to indignation to uncontrollable rage. He completely lost control. He was ready and even willing to fight physically.

Unknown to himself at that moment, the analysand was standing at the very center of the compensatory pattern of the unrelated masculine that had been unfolding in and around him for the past week. What he had witnessed in the play on the previous night was now his own reality. Just as the unrelated masculine had been suddenly released in the play, it burst into the foreground and was running rampant in the form of willfulness and obsession with principle. Like the Swiss policeman in the play, the pedestrian overreacted, not against the misdeed itself, but rather against the violation of principle; he and his friends had at no time been at risk of physical injury. Furthermore, just as the unrelated masculine coming through the Swiss policeman had released the diplomat's own unrelated side, the tirade of the male pedestrian similarly released the shadow in the analysand. The analysand had arrived at the hospital, and the "hair trigger" finger was on the button of nuclear war. Taken aback by the analysand's reaction, the pedestrian fortunately backed down and walked away, much as the Swiss policeman had done in the play.

As we have just seen, the journey toward conscious wholeness takes us not simply into the light, but also into the darkness. In order to change something inferior in ourselves, we must first see it in its fullness. Following the compensatory principle of like curing like, the analysand was led to see the dark depths of the unrelated masculine in himself through a synchronistic experience. What transpired certainly could have been worse, for far worse situations than this arise in connection with the unrelated masculine. The point is the context—the compensatory meaning in the confrontation with the male pedestrian. Being ethical means grasping that meaning, seeing it fully for what it really is, transforming ourselves by it, and consciously holding it in our lives.

The fundamental ideas about nature held by Jung and Freud were derived from their respective observations of the psyche, and therefore very much reflect their divergent conclusions. For Freud, civilization is needed to defend us against nature; for Jung, nature is needed to defend us against civilization. The "principal task of civilization," Freud reflects, "its actual *raison d'être*, is to defend us against nature." More specifically, the task of civilization is to defend us against the insatiable instincts residing in our own psyches. If released in the absence of the restrictions of civilization, our instincts would inevitably result in our destruction. Reflecting a view completely the converse of that held by Jung, Freud writes that nature would destroy us, "coldly, cruelly, relentlessly . . . possibly through the very things that occasioned our satisfaction."[15]

In striking contrast to Freud, Jung views nature as working relentlessly, not to bring about our destruction, but rather to lead us to experience wholeness in both the immediate and long-term sense. Nature is on our side, even though it doesn't always seem that way. Indeed, nature can appear to be very menacing, confronting us with our hidden aspects, with which we must necessarily come to terms if we are to become whole. The Jungian route is the way of descent as opposed to ascent. In spite of the very positive evaluation of nature that we find in this model, it is not an easy path to travel.

Alchemists sought their precious transformative stone in the dunghill where the "offensive" object had been flung in rejection by others. So, the success of analysis resides in the integration of the "rejected." The way of nature is the way of engaging, not of rising above, the truth of one's natural being. Paraphrasing the alchemist Morienus,[16] Maier writes: "Take that which is trodden underfoot in the dunghill, for if thou dost not, thou wilt fall on thine head when thou wouldst climb without steps." By way of interpretation, Jung adds, "if a man refuses to accept what he has spurned, it will recoil upon him the moment he wants to go higher."[17]

In Taoism, the bridge is a symbol of the split that has emerged between nature and culture. The bridge symbolizes our disengagement from nature, our desire to rise above it. More specifically, the bridge is a symbol of societal norms disengaging us from natural instincts which would bring us into relationship with nature as a whole.[18] The Taoist treatment of this symbol is supported by clinical dream material: (1) a person is driving a car toward a city. Having taken the wrong exit, he suddenly finds himself on a bridge carrying him over his intended destination; (2) another individual dreams of traveling across a bridge when it abruptly ends without warning, sending the analysand and vehicle plunging into the water below; (3) others struggle in vain to construct their own bridges out of materials such as newspapers—symbols of the societal or collective consciousness. Each time they attempt to walk over such bridges, they sink unsupported into the filthy river water below. Not unlike the rejected stone found on the dunghill, they must inevitably embrace this refuse if they are to become whole.

The way of nature and analysis is the way of descent. Accordingly, as one descends in the individuation process there are times when things appear unbearably dark. At these times, one must work very hard indeed to perceive and hold in consciousness the meaning that is struggling to come through. When Jung was waiting for equipment at an African railroad station, he had the good fortune to sit beside an Englishman who had spent 40 years in that country. Learning that Jung was new to Africa, the Englishman offered Jung some advice. "You know, Mister, this here is not man's country, it's God's country. So if anything should happen, just sit down and don't worry." Jung would never forget that advice, but would similarly advise his analysands who were destined to go deeply into their own psyches.[19] Very early in his work, Jung came to understand that no matter how dark things appear in the individuation process, all is taking place within a sacred circle of meaning—"God's country."

Perhaps Jung's most important clinical finding is that there exists in the psyche not only a point of orientation and meaning for the conscious personality, which he termed the "ego," but also a point of orientation and meaning for the whole conscious and unconscious psyche, which he termed the "self." Through his clinical observation of the compensatory activities of the psyche, Jung came to understand that the compensatory process works not simply to address day-to-day needs, but also to address more comprehensive developmental needs. This is especially true in the second half of life, where weighty questions about life and death close in on one, where a natural shift from more egocentric worldly problems toward transpersonal and archetypal, soul-level concerns takes place. As early as 1918, Jung noted that the self, as the archetype of orientation and meaning, is both the *spiritus rector*, director of this comprehensive developmental process, and the goal toward which the process is directed.[20] "I began to understand," Jung reflects in his memoirs, with reference to the years between 1918 and 1920, "that the goal of psychic development is the self. There is no linear evolution; there is only a circumambulation of the self."[21] Whether the individuation leads to the darkest depths of the shadow or to the fulfilment of relatedness, the self is always there, "summoned or not,"[22] offering guidance and protection through the compensatory activities of the unconscious.

I have explained elsewhere that what Jung discovered through his systematic study of the compensatory symbolisms of the unconscious and termed the archetype of the self is equivalent to what others have described as "God within."[23] When the theory of synchronicity comes into play, the archetypal or collective unconscious is not confined to the intrapsychic realm; having the same psychoid character that all archetypes possess,[24] the self should be understood as the equivalent not simply of "God within," but of "God without" as well.[25]

We move from a strictly inner world to what Jung describes as the psychoid, a subatomic world in which the psyche is co-extensive with nature as a whole, where the psychic and physical are one. With this theoretical progression, Jung leaps from theorizing about the nature of the psyche itself (metapsychology) to theorizing about the nature of reality (metaphysics). This progression is as legitimate as the former metapsychological theorizing about the self. In his treatment of the self as a metaphysical factor, Jung is simply giving theoretical expression to what he and others have clinically observed.[26]

As a metaphysical factor, the self strikingly parallels the descriptions of the Absolute that are found in the unitary worldviews of the Chinese and of the aboriginal peoples of North America. As in the synchronistic worldview, in these unitary worldviews there is no separation of the Absolute from nature, such as we find in the Bible. Similar to the Jungian description of the self, the descriptions of the Absolute in these nature-based worldviews are "not theological, but mythical—transtheological. The god, that is to say, is not a final term (like Yahweh), but the personification or agent of a power that is transcendent of deification and definition."[27] Making this same very critical point about the mythical nature of the self, Jung refers to the self as the totality of the archetypal or collective unconscious: "The collective unconscious, it's not for you, or me, it's the invisible world, it's the great spirit. It makes little difference what I call it: God, Tao, the Great Voice, the Great Spirit."[28]

In the synchronistic worldview, the sacred circle not only surrounds a person's individuation process, but also encompasses nature as a whole. To protect and guide the individuation process, the self reaches out not only through intrapsychic compensatory patterings, but also through synchronistic compensatory patterings. Both inwardly and outwardly, one is consciously led to follow a unique developmental pattern, a unique destiny.

When I was approaching the end of my Ph.D. work in England, I dreamt about a house on the street on which I grew up in Canada. No children lived in that house during the years of my childhood, so I knew nothing about it or its inhabitants. The house symbolized to me the unknown. As I moved toward the completion of my Ph.D., my sights were well focused on getting a full-time university teaching position. I especially remember an encounter I had with my external examiner following the completion of my doctorate. Dr. Robert Hobson, a senior Jungian medical analyst, had invited me to visit him in Manchester just before I was to return to Canada. On the day I visited, he advised me to go into clinical work as opposed to a university career. Following the completion of my M.A., I myself had been so inclined, but in the course of my Ph.D. work, I had shifted toward the academic route. As respectful as I was of Dr. Hobson's opinions, I did not allow his comments on this matter to penetrate.

When I returned from England to Canada, I was already short-listed and interviewing for teaching positions. With our young son, my wife and I went walking one day in the neighborhood of my childhood. As we turned onto the street on which I had lived, I saw the house of which I had dreamt in England. On the lawn were a woman and her young daughter raking leaves and twigs, cleaning up after the long winter. Knowing about synchronicity, I had to speak with her, to see if she could in any way inform me about the meaning of my dream. I kept the conversation going for a good 20 minutes. The only thing that stood out to me was that she was from Toronto, where I was being considered for a position. Perhaps, I thought, I was merely intended to hear horror stories of the cost of living in that city.

Several weeks passed, but I was offered no full-time academic position. Having been so determined about the course things would take, I was devastated. On the other hand, I was now able to sit down and hear what Dr. Hobson had been trying to tell me in Manchester. Approximately three months later, I began clinical work under the direction of a psychologist. Shortly after I joined her practice, we had to move offices, due to the sale of the site of our existing office. I was looking in the north of the city, she in the south. She called me one day to say that she had found what seemed like the perfect place. Only days before, I had selected an apartment for my family just around the corner from it. Not too long after we moved into our new office, I went to speak with the owner of the building. As we ended our discussion, he took me into an adjoining room to meet his secretary, who was also his wife. When she stood up from her desk to greet me, I recognized her, as she did me. She was the woman I had stopped to speak with, who had been raking the leaves in front of the house on the street where I grew up, which I had dreamt about in England.

There are a number of important things to say about this synchronistic experience. The dream in England was the potential point of access to a pattern that would be of great significance for my life. Had I not recorded that dream, and had I then not followed through with my investigation, I would have lost the meaning of what was unfolding in the larger picture. The house symbolized the unknown, and certainly the destiny that would be fulfilled in relation to that symbol was completely unknown to me, even as I spoke with the woman who was raking the leaves on that spring day. My intention had been to pursue the academic route that would necessarily take me out of the city of my birth; the house was the symbol of the unforeseen shift to clinical work that would occur in the city of my birth.

Related to this, during a particularly intense period of inner work a few years before I went to England, I had cast the I Ching and been given hexagram 24. This hexagram, which is titled the Return, held tremendous significance for me from that time. The number of the "unknown" house was 24, something of a play on this idea of the Return.

I would like to offer a few reflections with respect to the question of destiny. Some individuals take the position that at the end of their lives they will necessarily arrive at the place to which they are intended. To my mind, the above example does not support such a conclusion, nor does it suggest that the future is predictable in the sense of foreseeing a necessarily fixed destiny. The dream in England was rather providing me with a glimpse of the direction things might take if I were to follow one particular path—one of countless courses of action open to me. I believed that the specific path the dream revealed would best lead me toward the realization of my potential as an individual. The dream revealed what I might call the

Tao of my life. The greatest obstacle to bringing my life into conscious relationship to the Tao is what I term "ego control," the ego's refusal to give up its wrong conclusions drawn on its too limited understanding of things. Certainly, a good portion of many lives has been wasted away waiting for the wrong doors to open. In contrast to ego control is ego strength, which puts the ego in service of the self, enabling one to "[endure] the truth, and . . . [cope] with the world and with fate," as Jung relates, even when "incomprehensible things happen."[29]

Both inwardly, and outwardly through the compensatory patternings in nature, the self surrounds the individuation process in a sacred circle of meaning. Personal and transpersonal meanings flow together as the totality seeks conscious manifestation in the life of the individual through its compensatory activities. We are at once led and must lead. This is not exclusively a question of divine Grace, nor is it one of works alone. The covenant is unconditional and everlasting—nature's compensatory workings are relentless and keep coming at us until we get it right. On the other hand, there is no vicarious atonement, for no one can take the place of the individual who alone must be the one to walk the path. Through ego strength, not ego control, the whole self which strives for conscious realization in our being becomes Incarnate. Through such Incarnation, creation is supported and furthered.

The heightened consciousness to which the unitary synchronistic worldview calls us is reflected in the visionary works of the English poet William Blake (1757–1827). In his "Auguries of Innocence," Blake writes: "To see a World in a Grain of Sand/And a Heaven in a Wild Flower,/Hold Infinity in the palm of your hand/And Eternity in an hour."[30] Here, as in the synchronistic worldview, the particular is the point of access to the totality, the self. This, too, is the consciousness of the non-dualistic perspective of Zen Buddhism, which experiences nature and human beings not as separated, but as co-existing in the same unified field of the Buddha-mind.[31] One of the most widely cited descriptions of this non-dualistic consciousness is from the Zen poet Basho (1643–1694), whom Suzuki describes as the "founder of the modern school of *haiku*."[32] In the Japanese, the text reads: "Furu ike ya/Kawazu tobikomu/Mizu no oto." Suzuki's English version reads: "The old pond, ah!/A frog jumps in: The water's sound!"[33] Moving away from Suzuki's literal translation, Noss attempts to seize the spirit of the poem: "An old pond, mirror still./A quick frog, slanting waterward./A liquid *plop!*"[34] In the non-dualistic consciousness of Zen, the poet is not simply an observer of what is taking place; rather, he is part of it. The "plop!" therefore, is the sound of the poet himself entering the water.[35] Through the particular conscious access to the self as totality, the Buddha-nature is opened. This is an ethical response of the highest order. In our relation to the compensatory workings of nature as a whole, we choose between consciousness and unconsciousness, progression and regression. At every turn, in apparently isolated and seemingly insignificant events, we face ethical decisions of far-reaching significance. Everything hinges on how we hold the meaning of the unfoldment of nature in our consciousness and in our lives.

The spiritual crisis of the twenty-first century will not be addressed by turning our gaze exclusively toward the inner world, as Jungian psychology to date has largely counseled. Our experience of loss of soul stems in part from our outward separation from nature as a spiritual reality. An exclusive focus on the inner world cannot address this problem. Freud and Jung searched for the soul by situating ultimate meaning exclusively within the psyche. This constitutes the dispensation of the twentieth century. In the twenty-first century, the search for soul will require a development of the works of Freud and Jung that will close the sacred circle on inner and outer nature. This consciousness will re-connect us with nature outwardly as a spiritual reality through the depths of our inner beings. This will be the contribution of the synchronistic worldview.

NOTES

1. Robert Aziz, *C. G. Jung's Psychology of Religion and Synchronicity* (Albany, NY: State University of New York Press, 1990), pp. 9–10.

2. Mircea Eliade, *Shamanism: Archaic Techniques of Ecstasy*, trans. Willard R. Trask (Princeton, NJ: Princeton University Press, 1964), pp. 3–8.

3. Marie-Louise von Franz, *C. G. Jung: His Myth in Our Time*, trans. William H. Kennedy (London: Hodder & Stoughton, 1975), p. 13.

4. C. G. Jung, Foreword to Neumann's *Depth Psychology and a New Ethic, Collected Works* (hereafter cited as *C.W.*), vol. 18, trans. R. F. C. Hull (Princeton, NJ: Princeton University Press, 1976), par. 1416, p. 619.

5. *The Layman's Parallel Bible* (Grand Rapids, MI: ZonderVan Bible Publishers, 1973), King James Version, p. 4.

6. C. G. Jung, *Mysterium Coniunctionis, C.W.*, vol. 14, trans. R. F. C. Hull (Princeton, NJ: Princeton University Press, 1976), par. 756, p. 531.

7. Ferne Jensen, ed., *C. G. Jung, Emma Jung and Toni Wolff: A Collection of Remembrances* (San Francisco: The Analytical Psychology Club of San Francisco, 1982), p. 21.

8. William McGuire, ed., *Dream Analysis: Notes of the Seminar Given in 1928–1930 by C. G. Jung* (London: Routledge & Kegan Paul, 1984), pp. 43–45.

9. Richard Wilhelm, *The Secret of the Golden Flower*, trans. from the German by Cary F. Baynes, commentary by C. G. Jung (New York: Harcourt, Brace & World, 1962), pp. 138ff.

10. The principal paper "Synchronizität als ein Prinzip akausaler Zusammenhänge," was published together with a monograph by W. Pauli entitled "Der Einfluss archetypischer Vorstellungen auf die Bildung naturwissenschaftlicher Theorien bei Kepler" in the volume *Naturerklärung und Psyche* (Studien aus dem C. G. Jung-Institut, IV; Zurich, 1952). This volume was translated as *The Interpretation of Nature and Psyche* (New York [Bollingen Series LI] and London, 1955). See editor's

note in C. G. Jung, "Synchronicity: An Acausal Connecting Principle," *C.W.*, vol. 8, trans. R. F. C. Hull (Princeton, NJ: Princeton University Press, 1978), p. 417 and par. 816, p. 419.

11. C. G. Jung, *Memories, Dreams, Reflections*, recorded and edited by Aniela Jaffé, trans. Richard and Clara Winston (New York: Vintage Books, 1965), p. 192.

12. *The Secret of the Golden Flower*, p. 118.

13. Carol Gilligan, *In a Different Voice: Psychological Theory and Women's Development* (Cambridge, MA: Harvard University Press, 1982).

14. C. G. Jung, ed., *Man and His Symbols* (Garden City, NY: Doubleday, 1979), p. 85.

15. Sigmund Freud, "The Future of an Illusion," *Works of Sigmund Freud, Standard Edition*, vol. 21, trans. James Strachey (London: Hogarth Press, 1961), p. 15.

16. C. G. Jung, "Individual Dream Symbolism in Relation to Alchemy," *C.W.*, vol. 12, trans. R. F. C. Hull (Princeton, NJ: Princeton University Press, 1977), par. 386, p. 272. Note 88, p. 272, reads, "Morienus (Morienes or Marianus) is said to have been the teacher of Omayyad prince, Kalid or Khalid ibn-Jazid ibn-Muawiyah" (635–704).

17. C. G. Jung, "Religious Ideas in Alchemy," *C.W.*, vol. 12, par. 514 and n. 205, p. 430.

18. Herbert A. Giles, *Chuang Tzu: Taoist Philosopher and Chinese Mystic* (London: George Allen & Unwin., 1961), p. 98.

19. Barbara Hannah, *Jung: His Life and Work* (New York: G. P. Putnam's Sons, 1976), p. 172.

20. Aziz, op. cit., pp. 21–22.

21. C. G. Jung, *Memories, Dreams, Reflections*, p. 196.

22. Above the door of his home in Küsnacht, Jung had carved in stone the following pronouncement attributed to the Delphic Oracle: "VOCATUS ATQUE NON VOCATUS DEUS ADERIT" ("Summoned or not, the god will be there"). Aniela Jaffé, ed., *C. G. Jung: Word and Image*, trans. Krishna Winston (Princeton, NJ: Princeton University Press, 1979), p. 136.

23. Aziz, op. cit., pp. 17ff.

24. Ibid., pp. 51ff.

25. Ibid., pp. 180ff.

26. Ibid., pp. 173ff.

27. Joseph Campbell, *The Way of the Animal Powers: Historical Atlas of World Mythology*, vol. 1 (London: Times Books, 1984), pp. 193–194.

28. William McGuire and R. F. C. Hull, eds., *C. G. Jung Speaking: Interviews and Encounters* (London: Pan Books, 1980), p. 375.

29. C. G. Jung, *Memories, Dreams, Reflections*, p. 297.

30. William Blake, "Auguries of Innocence," in Richard Wilbur, ed., *Blake* (New York: Dell, 1973), pp. 99–102.

31. John B. Noss, *Man's Religions* (New York: Macmillan, 1974), pp. 169–170. Reprinted with permission.

32. Daisetz T. Suzuki, *Zen and Japanese Culture* (Princeton, NJ: Princeton University Press, 1973), p. 227. Reprinted with permission.

33. Ibid., p. 227.

34. Noss, op. cit., pp. 169–170.

35. Ibid., p. 170.

REFERENCES

Aziz, Robert. 1990. *C. G. Jung's Psychology of Religion and Synchronicity*. Albany: State University of New York Press.

Campbell, Joseph. 1984. *The Way of the Animal Powers*. London: Times Books.

Eliade, Mircea. 1964. *Shamanism: Archaic Techniques of Ecstasy*. Willard R. Trask, trans. Princeton, NJ: Princeton University Press.

Giles, Herbert A. 1961. *Chuang Tzu: Taoist Philosopher and Chinese Mystic*. London: George Allen & Unwin.

Gilligan, Carol. 1982. *In a Different Voice: Psychological Theory and Women's Development*. Cambridge, MA: Harvard University Press.

Hannah, Barbara. 1976. *Jung: His Life and Work*. New York: G. P. Putnam's Sons.

Jaffé, Aniela, (ed.). 1979. *C. G. Jung: Word and Image*. Krishna Winston, trans. Princeton, NJ: Princeton University Press.

Jensen, Ferne (ed.). 1982. *C. G. Jung, Emma Jung, and Toni Wolff*. San Francisco: Analytical Psychology Club of San Francisco.

Jung, Carl Gustav. 1955. *The Interpretation of Nature and Psyche*. New York: Bollingen.

Jung, Carl Gustav. 1965. *Memories, Dreams, Reflections*. Aniela Jaffé, ed., Richard and Clara Winston, trans. New York: Vintage.

Jung, Carl Gustav. 1976. *Collected Works (C.W.)*. R. F. C. Hull, trans. Princeton, NJ: Princeton University Press.

Jung, Carl Gustav. 1979. *Man and His Symbols*. Garden City, NY: Doubleday.

McGuire, William, and R. F. C. Hull (eds.). 1980. *C. G. Jung Speaking: Interviews and Encounters*. London: Pan Books.

McGuire, William (ed.). 1984. *Dream Analysis: Notes of the Seminar Given in 1928–1930 by C. G. Jung*. London: Routledge & Kegan Paul.

Noss, John B. 1974. *Man's Religions*. New York: Macmillan.

Suzuki, Daisetz T. 1973. *Zen and Japanese Culture*. Princeton, NJ: Princeton University Press.

von Franz, Marie-Louise. 1975. *C. G. Jung: His Myth in Our Time*. William H. Kennedy, trans. London: Hodder & Stoughton.

Wilbur, Richard (ed.). 1973. *Blake*. New York: Dell.

Wilhelm, Richard. 1962. *The Secret of the Golden Flower*. Cary F. Baynes, trans.; C. G. Jung, commentary. New York: Harcourt, Brace & World.

5

Loving the World as Our Own Body: The Non-dualist Ethics of Taoism, Buddhism, and Deep Ecology

DAVID R. LOY

In the last decade or so, ethics has experienced a revolution, as the parameters basic to ethical debate since ancient Greece have been transformed. Until quite recently, the problem of ethics has been what binds us human beings together: how to relate to other people, or to society as a whole, without using or abusing each other. Today the issue of ethical responsibility has broadened to encompass the whole ecosphere. The crucial question has become how to relate to *all* beings, not only animals and plants but also apparently non-sentient "beings" such as tropical rain forest systems and the ozone layer. In spite of distractions such as the debate over "sustainable development," the suspicion continues to grow that what is involved is much more than merely the need to preserve "our natural resources." Lynn White, Jr., one of the first to consider the philosophical implications of the ecological crisis, realized that the issue is fundamentally a spiritual one: "Since the roots of our trouble are so largely religious, the remedy must also be essentially religious, whether we call it that or not. We must rethink and refeel our destiny."[1] It is becoming obvious that what is required is nothing less than a fundamental transformation in the way we have understood the relation between ourselves and the earth.

At the heart of this issue, we are also beginning to realize, is *the self*. The ecological problem seems to be the perennial personal problem writ large: a consequence of the alienation between myself and the world I find myself "in." "The same dualism that reduces things to objects for consciousness is at work in the humanism that reduces nature to raw material for mankind."[2] In both these dualisms, the self is understood to be the locus of awareness and therefore the source of meaning and value. This devalues the objective world, including all of nature, into merely that sphere of activity wherein the self labors to fulfil itself. The alienated subject feels no responsibility for the objectified other and attempts to find satisfaction through exploitative projects which, in fact, usually increase the sense of alienation. The meaning and purpose that we seek can be attained only by establishing a more non-dual relationship with the objectified other: in ecological terms, with the earth which is not only our home but our mother. In contrast to the main humanistic or "anthropocentric" tendency within the West, Asian philosophical and religious traditions have had much to say about the non-duality of subject and object. As a small contribution to the debate, this chapter will discuss and compare the relevant insights of Taoism, Buddhism, and deep ecology. All three of these perspectives avoid the usual is/ought problem (how to infer what one *should* do from what *is* the case—a category mistake) by transposing the issue from morality to understanding: the main problem is not evil but ignorance, and the solution is not primarily a matter of applying the will but of reaching an insight into the nature of things. Socrates is vindicated: immoral conduct is indeed due to ignorance, for if we really knew the good, we would do it. The catch, of course, is in the *really*, for the type of knowledge necessary is neither the correct moral code nor any objective scientific understanding, but an insight which can liberate us from the dualistic ways of thinking whereby we "bind ourselves without a rope."

TAOISM

> The reason why we have trouble is that we have a body. When we have no body, what trouble do we have? Therefore: he who loves the whole world as if it were his own body can be trusted with the whole world.
>
> *Tao Te Ching*, ch. 13

The Taoist critique of the self opposes self-ness with the realization of Tao, which is neither a transcendental God nor an impersonal Absolute but the dynamic source from which all natural phenomena arise. Formless, invisible, soundless, immaterial, unhindered, imperturbable, Tao is "the form of the formless, the image of the imageless," empty (*ch'ung*) and apparently inexhaustible (*Tao Te Ching*, ch. 14, 4). The relationship between it and the many things in the world is described using such metaphors as the nave and spokes of a wheel, the space inside a pot, the door and windows to a room—whose emptiness is not a lack but necessary for the wheel, pot and room to function (*Tao Te Ching*, ch. 11). We can never objectively *grasp* such emptiness, yet it is necessary for anything to be—or more precisely, for anything to happen, since Taoism and Buddhism both reject a substance-based ontology in favor of an event-based process one.

To experience Tao is to realize that humans are not exceptions to this natural process, for we too are manifestations of it. Instead of being the crown of creation, at the top of a great chain of beings, *Homo sapiens* is only one of the ten thousand things which the Tao treats indifferently, like the straw dogs used in ceremonies and then thrown away (*Tao Te Ching*, ch. 5). The ten thousand things are related not vertically, with those of lesser value supporting those of higher value, but horizontally, all being citizens in the great commonwealth that is the natural world. This attitude may make us uncomfortable—who likes to lose their special status?—but it is all the more noteworthy because it will recur later in this chapter. For Mahayana Buddhism, too, all beings are equally "empty" (*sunya*) because they all lack self-existence. And what has been called the central insight of deep ecology is "the idea that we can make no firm ontological divide in the field of existence: That there is no bifurcation in reality between the human and the non-human realms."[3] If so, this realization constitutes a revolution of consciousness perhaps no less significant than that of Copernicus and Darwin. Copernicus displaced the earth from its divinely-allocated position as the center of creation; Darwin demonstrated that we too are a product of the same evolutionary forces that created other species, but (whether or not this was his intention) that still seemed to leave humans the ultimate victors in the struggle for life. Now that our privileged status becomes questionable, where does that leave us?

Several passages in the *Tao Te Ching* allude to the need to overcome subject-object duality (e.g., chs. 7 and 13, the latter the epigraph to this section). As we would expect from a later and more discursive work, the other Taoist classic, the *Chuang-tzu*, is less ambiguous in asserting that "the perfect man has no self": "If there is no other, there will be no I. If there is no I, there will be none to make distinctions."[4]

It is because there is right, that there is wrong; it is because there is wrong, that there is right. This being the situation, the sages do not approach things at this level, but reflect the light of nature. Thereupon the self is also the other; the other is also the self. . . . But really are there such distinctions as the self and the other, or are there no such distinctions? *When the self and the other lose their contrariety, there we have the very essence of the Tao.*[5]

This denial of the duality between self and other is a striking claim: so strange, so counter-intuitive, that we are not sure how to take it; yet the fact that it is a common claim in the mainstream Asian traditions suggests we should consider it quite seriously. Its ethical implications were realized early in Indian Vedanta: "He who sees all beings as the very Self and the Self in all beings in consequence of that abhors none" (*Isa Upanisad*, verse 6). Vidyaranya put it even better: "The knowledge of the Self leads to the identification of oneself with others as clearly as one identifies with one's own body."[6] This brings us back to chapter 13 of the *Tao Te Ching*, which

also recommends loving the whole world as if it were one's own body. . . .
And what if it *is* our body? What if the discrimination we usually make
between our own body and the rest of the world is a delusion, as Advaita
Vedanta, Buddhism and Taoism claim? Such a realization would certainly
have far-reaching ethical implications—more important, perhaps, than any
other fact about the world.

Everyone agrees that the most important chapter of the *Tao Te Ching* is
the first one; some scholars (e.g., Chung-yuan Chang and Wing-tsit Chan)
claim it is the key to the entire work and that all the chapters which follow
may be inferred from it. Unfortunately this opening passage is also notoriously obscure. If my non-dualist interpretation of Taoism is correct, we
would expect the first chapter to say something important about the relation between subject-object dualism and a more non-dualistic way of experiencing the world. In fact, that is exactly what the chapter seems to be
about: lines 1, 3, 5, and 7 refer to the non-dual Tao; lines 2, 4, 6, and 8
to our usual dualistic way of experiencing ourselves "in" the world:

> The Tao that can be Tao'd is not the constant Tao
> The name that can be named is not a constant name
> Having-no-name is the source of heaven and earth
> Having-names is the mother of the ten thousand things
> Therefore when you do not have intention you can see the wonder
> When you have intention you see the forms
> These two things have the same origin
> Although different in name . . .

Without going into a detailed analysis of these lines, which would take
us beyond the scope of this chapter,[7] they may be summarized as follows.
The odd-numbered lines describe the nameless Tao, the source of heaven
and earth, which is the world apprehended as a "spiritual" whole. Such
Tao-experience can occur when one has no intentions (*yu*), in which case
there is no awareness of oneself as being other than the Tao. In contrast,
the even-numbered lines refer to our usual and dualistic way of experiencing the world, perceiving it as a collection of interacting yet discrete objects
including ourselves. We experience the world in this way due to names
(language) and intentions, mental processes which are not the activities that
a self does but rather are what sustain the illusory sense of a self separate
from the world it is supposed to be "in."

What is the problem with language and intentions? Naming divides up
the world into many different things; then we wonder about how they (and
we!) fit together. But the Tao is not a collection of things, as the *Chuang-tzu*
emphasizes:

The knowledge of the ancients was perfect. How perfect? At first, they did not
know that there were things. This is the most perfect knowledge; nothing can be

added. Next, they knew that there were things, but did not yet make distinctions between them. Next they made distinctions among them, but they did not yet pass judgments upon them. When judgments were passed, Tao was destroyed.[8]

From the Taoist perspective (and the Buddhist, which also emphasizes impermanence), the alternative to discrete things is events and processes. Everything is in motion, in transformation, and all those movements constitute a great flux in which everything harmonizes.

We cannot appreciate this alternative to intentions until we understand the problem with intentions, a problem that is becoming worse in contemporary society: the infinite regress of a life which relates to everything as a means to something else. Today children in Japan (where I write this) take entrance exams for kindergarten, because the right kindergarten will help them get into the right primary school which will help them get into the right middle school which will help them get into the right high school which will help them get into the right university which will help them get hired by the right corporation. So much for childhood! In his old age the poet W. B. Yeats reflected: "When I think of all the books I have read, wise words heard, anxieties given to parents, . . . of hopes I have had, all life weighed in the balance of my own life seems to me *a preparation for something that never happens*."[9] As the world becomes more organized and rationalized (in Weber's sense), that becomes ever more true. The romantic yearning for a "return to nature" gains much of its attraction from the fact that in modern bureaucratized society less and less is done for its own sake.

This helps us to understand the Taoist alternative to such an intention-ridden infinite regress: spontaneity (*tzu-jan*) or "self-creativity," is based on the realization that *all things, including us, flourish by themselves*. Today we have difficulty appreciating this because we lack the crucial insight that spontaneity is not opposed to order but is an expression of it, since it arises from the unforced unfolding of that natural order. For us, spontaneity is by definition a lack of order because our order is a function of reason: something to be logically understood and imposed on things. Instead of attempting to control (ourselves, other people, the world), Taoism emphasises *letting-go*. We learn by accumulating knowledge, but we lose our *self*-consciousness and realize the Tao by "reducing" ourselves again and again, until we reach *wei-wu-wei*, the "action of non-action": then, although one does nothing, nothing is left undone (ch. 48).

Wei-wu-wei is the central paradox of Taoism and notoriously difficult to understand—until we realize that what is being recommended is not literally doing-nothing, but non-dual action: that is, action without the sense of an agent-self who is apart from the action and who experiences herself as the one doing it. The usual interpretations of *wu-wei*—non-interference and passively yielding—view not-acting as a kind of action, whereas non-dual action reverses this and sees non-action—that which does not change, a stillness that is not lost—"in" a non-dual action. Again, it is significant that the same paradox is found in other Asian traditions which maintain the non-duality of subject and object, particularly in Mahayana Buddhism. For example, Niu-t'ou Fa-yung, a Buddhist teacher, expressed the same insight using the Ch'an concept of "no mind": "The moment when the mind is in action is the moment at which no-mind acts. . . . No-mind is that which is in action; it is that constant action which does not act."[10] The Taoist denies that I *act*, the Buddhist denies that *I* act; but they amount to the same thing, since each half of the polarity is dependent on the other. As long as there is the sense of oneself as an agent distinct from one's action, there will be a sense of action due to the relation between them. When one *is* the action, no residue of self-consciousness remains to observe that action objectively. So the way to transcend the duality between subject and object is to *be* the act, in which case one realizes that it is not the self that acts but the Tao that manifests through oneself, or better (because less dualistic), *as* oneself. Then there is *wu-wei*: a quiet center that does not change while activity constantly and spontaneously occurs, a situation Chuang-tzu calls "tranquility-in-disturbance." In this way we re-achieve the simplicity of a child who is "free from marks [characteristics]" and "does not take credit" for what she does (ch. 22) because she does not have the sense of a self that does them. It is when we live in this fashion that all things flourish by themselves.

We seem to have drifted away from ethics, but the Taoist approach to morality follows directly from this nondualistic way of living (in) the world. The long passage quoted above from the *Chuang-tzu* begins: "It is because there is right, that there is wrong; it is because there is wrong, that there is right. This being the situation, the sages do not approach things at this level, but reflect the light of nature." The *Tao Te Ching* makes the same point: "When all know beauty acting as beauty, then only there is ugliness. When all know good acting as good, then only there is not-good. For being and non-being are mutually produced . . . " (ch. 2). This is another mode of nondualism (also important in Mahayana Buddhism); a critique of *dualistic thinking* that differentiates things into opposed categories: right versus wrong, beauty versus ugliness, being versus nonbeing, life versus death, success versus failure, and so forth. It has often been pointed out that instead of either/or—the Western logic of *tertium non datur*—Chinese thought emphasises polarity (e.g., *yin/yang*). But the Taoist critique of dualistic thinking is more than a preference for polarities. Dualistic thinking is delusive; we discriminate between opposites because we want to have one term and reject the other, yet that is impossible because each term gains meaning only by being the opposite of the other. This means, for example, that someone who wants to be beautiful will be preoccupied with avoiding ugliness; that our hope for success equals our fear of failure; that to cling to life is actually to be obsessed with death. Such a dichotomizing way of thinking *about* a situation keeps us from *being* the situation; it is a classic example of the kind of conceptual thinking that needs to be "reduced again and again"—that is, let go.

Then what about the distinction we make between right and wrong, between good and evil? Isn't *that* dualism necessary for any ethics at all? Aldous Huxley makes the case for this view:

Evil is the accentuation of division; good, whatever makes for unity with other lives and other beings. Pride, hatred, anger—the essentially evil sentiments: and essentially evil because they are all intensifications of the given reality of separateness, because they insist upon division and uniqueness, because they reject and deny other lives and beings.[11]

For Huxley, evil is that which promotes separation, good is that which promotes unity. But then isn't it inconsistent to accentuate the division between *them*? Doesn't his distinction between good and evil intensify separateness and division, by rejecting and denying the life of those things we label as evil? This becomes more than a logical point when we remember how much evil has been created by our desire to eliminate evil. The cultural psychoanalyst Otto Rank believed that our greatest human problems and sufferings are due, ironically, to the human attempt to *perfect* the world. Medieval inquisitors burned thousands at the stake in order to purge Christendom of heresies spread by Satan; Stalin sacrificed millions to construct his ideal socialist state; Hitler's Final Solution to the Jewish Problem was an attempt to purify the earth. All these horrible deeds were justified as necessary to rid the world of evil!

This helps us to appreciate the full import of the Taoist (and Buddhist) critique of dualistic thinking: *To let go of such discriminations means to let go of dualistic moral codes as well.* This is not an excuse for selfishness, for the point is that a genuine "reduction" will also eliminate those self-centered ways of thinking which motivate selfish behavior. Deeper than the imperfectly-flexible strictures of moral codes is the concern for others that springs up spontaneously within those who have realized the Tao, because such self-less persons no longer feel separate from "others." That is why the way to get rid of our body (self), which causes us such trouble, is to realize that the whole world is our body, in which case we can be entrusted with the world. The Taoist critique of Confucianism follows from this:

When the great Tao declines, we have (the teaching of) benevolence and righteousness . . .

When the six family relations are not friendly, we have (the teaching of) filial piety and paternal affection.

When the state and its families are confused and out of order, there are (the teachings of) loyalty and faithfulness. (ch. 18)

For Taoism, Confucian emphasis on benevolence and righteousness is an attempt to close the barn door of morality after the horse of natural feeling has already run away. As Nietzsche realized, such moral codes are ultimately motivated by fear, which makes us want to control both others and ourselves. The alternative to that fear is nothing other than *love*, something which, if it is to be genuine, no moral code can legislate. What is the foundation or basis of love? The classic example is that of a mother for her child, who was part of her and even after birth cannot survive without her. Perhaps what we understand as love is the affective aspect of a nondual ontological realization: the experience that I am not-other-than the beloved.

This is consistent with the insight that concludes Spinoza's *Ethics*: blessedness is not the reward of virtue but virtue itself. A life filled with love is blessed not because it leads to some other reward, but because a life of love, which unites us with others, is blessedness itself. The other side of this is that a life which lacks love is not punishment for evil but evil itself. From a non-dualist perspective, we are not punished *for* our sins but *by* them. To lack love is to feel separate from the world, and the tragedy is that this lack encourages us to do things which further aggravate our sense of duality; those who attempt to manipulate the world for their own advantage increasingly alienate themselves from it. Such people cannot help expecting the same attitude from others, leading to a life based on fear and to the need to control situations. This vicious circle can lead to a hellish solipsism, and in fact solipsism is as good a definition of hell as we have.

Such is the Taoist perspective on personal ethics; but does Taoism have something more to say about human society today, at the end of the twentieth century? Our technological "global village" is so far removed from the hamlets of Lao-tzu and Chuang-tzu that we may doubt it, yet Lao and Chuang still speak directly to our social condition. The ecological crisis forces us to recognize that the crucial issue of our time is the relation between the fragile biosphere and our limitless technological drive to dominate the natural world and make it serve our own purposes. The Taoist critique addresses this, for in place of the *intentions* that keep us preoccupied with "improving" the world, that imply a future-orientation that is always going somewhere (but is unable ever to rest anywhere), Taoism suggests *wei-wu-wei* and letting things be. When we plug this critique into our global situation today, its relevance becomes obvious: our contemporary emphasis on endless economic and technological development is a collective example of the future-oriented intentionality which needs to interfere with the world, because it is unable to be one with it; and the natural world that we are destroying in the process is the sphere of *wu-wei* and letting things be. In place of its spontaneity and self-creativity, we are obsessed with organizing and "improving" it; when we look at the Amazon and other rain forests, we see only vast "resources" waiting to be "exploited." To what end? Where are we trying to get so fast? Our tragedy is that growth has become an end in itself, even as that growth threatens to destroy us.

An attitude to life that seeks fulfilment in the single-minded pursuit of wealth—in short, materialism—does not fit into this world, because it contains within itself no limiting principle, while the environment in which it is placed is strictly limited.[12]

If in the future we are to live together peacefully in an over-populated world, we must come to appreciate the Taoist emphasis on simple pleasures and fewer desires.

The irony is that the more we try to control situations, the more disorder is created—precisely what Taoism implies. This is not some mystical claim, but is increasingly obvious in the way our technological solutions to problems (e.g., the need for large amounts of electric power) keep creating ecological disasters (Three Mile Island, Chernobyl). For that reason it is difficult to be hopeful about the technological solutions that have been proposed for those disasters. A new approach is needed, and I suspect that any solution which is successful will embody an appreciation of the Taoist insight into the self-organizing spontaneity of the natural world.

BUDDHISM

> I came to realize clearly that mind is no other than mountains and rivers and the great wide earth, the sun and the moon and the stars.
>
> Zen master Dogen[13]

From its beginnings, Buddhism has emphasized ethics. In what is believed to have been the first sermon, Sakyamuni Buddha summarized his teaching into four truths: *dukkha* (usually translated "suffering"), the cause of *dukkha* (desire), the end of *dukkha* (nirvana), and the eightfold path that leads to the end of *dukkha*: right understanding, right thought, right speech, right action, right livelihood, right effort, right mindfulness, and right meditation. The eightfold path is often grouped into the three pillars of *sila* (morality), *samadhi* (meditation), and *prajña* (wisdom or insight). *Sila* is regarded as providing the moral and karmic foundation necessary both for lay life and for successful meditation and enlightenment.

Five ethical precepts are commonly abstracted from the eightfold path: to avoid killing, stealing, false speech, "sensuality," and intoxicants. No-

table from an ecological perspective is that the precept against killing protects not only humans but all sentient beings. Sensuality means
preoccupation with sense-pleasures generally, yet it is usually understood
as improper sex; "you should avoid sex that will cause pain and suffering
to others," as it has sometimes been expressed. In Buddhism marriage and
divorce are not religious but civil matters; Buddhism does not say that
divorce is wrong. (There is also no prohibition against contraception, although abortion may violate the rule against killing.)

From a Western viewpoint, what is most interesting about the precepts
is that they are not commandments imposed upon us by the Buddha or
some god, but *undertakings* that we choose to impose upon ourselves. "I
undertake the course of training to perfect myself in the precept of not
killing," etc. Even while reciting them we know that we will violate them,
yet we vow to continue the attempt to embody them as the basic principles
of our conduct in the world. The idea behind this perspective is the belief
that it is we ourselves who suffer the most when we break the precepts.

Another simpler version of the precepts originates from a verse in the
Dhammapada, that most popular of Buddhist texts: "Renounce all evil,
practice all good, keep the mind pure; thus all the Buddhas have taught."[14]
Mahayana Buddhism expanded this to emphasize the attitude of the *bodhisattva*, who takes on the responsibility to help all sentient beings attain
salvation: "Renounce all evil, practice all good, save the many beings." The
first of the four vows still recited daily in all Zen temples embodies the
same approach: "Although living beings are numberless, I vow to save them
all." The ten basic Mahayana precepts add five more to the Pali precepts:
not to discuss the faults of others, not to praise oneself while abusing others, not to spare the *dharma* assets, not to indulge in anger, and not to
defame the three treasures (Buddha, *dharma, sangha*). These five add a
greater psychological sensitivity to the ways the ego-sense protects and per-
petuates itself.

To these ten precepts the path of the *bodhisattva* adds six *paramitas*:
generosity, morality, patience, exertion, meditation, and wisdom (*prajña*).
Paramita, usually translated as "transcendental" (transcendental generosity, etc.) or "perfection of" (perfection of generosity, etc.), literally means
"to go beyond," and refers to character traits developed to the highest
possible degree. Generosity (*dana*) is first for good reason; it is the pre-
eminent Buddhist virtue, emphasised more in Buddhism than in any other
religion; some teachers have said that it contains all the other virtues. Buddhism like Taoism condemns the practice of performing good deeds with
expectation of material reward or respect, because transcendental generosity denies the barrier between the one who gives and the one who receives. Accordingly, Mahayana emphasizes that *dana-paramita* is
generosity without any awareness that it is oneself who is giving, that there
is another who receives, or even that there is a gift which is given. A very

similar insight is found in the *Tao Te Ching*: "Not being self-boasting, therefore one has merit" (ch. 22). "Superior virtue (*te*) is no virtue, therefore it has virtue. Inferior virtue does not lose its virtue, therefore it has no virtue" (ch. 38). As long as I am aware of my generosity, that generosity is not complete: something extra remains or "sticks," which therefore does not reduce the sense-of-self but aggravates it.

The eighth-century Buddhist poet and philosopher Santideva reminds us of the non-dualist perspective that grounds this approach to ethics: "Those who wish to bring themselves and others swiftly to salvation should perform the supreme act of converting others into oneself."[15] As this suggests, Buddhist morality cannot be comprehended apart from such a realization, which liberates us from the sufferings (*dukkha*) inherent in a sense of self. In order to understand Buddhist ethics, we must consider its foundation in the Buddhist understanding of the self—or more precisely, the Buddhist deconstruction of the self, since the denial of self is essential to Buddhism and one of its most distinguishing features.

Like Taoism, Buddhism is sensitive to how language reifies things and causes us to perceive the world as a collection of self-existing (*svabhava*) objects "in" objectified space and time. The central insight of Buddhism is a critique of this tendency: not only a denial of ego-self but a critique of *all* self-existing "thingness." This is the point of *pratitya-samutpada* "dependent-origination," the most important Buddhist doctrine. (The Buddha emphasised that anyone who really understands *pratitya-samutpada* understands his teaching, and vice versa.)

"Dependent-origination" explains our experience by locating all phenomena within a set of twelve factors, each conditioned by all the others and likewise conditioning all of them. The presupposition of the whole process is (1) *ignorance*, due to which (2) *volitional tendencies* affect (3) *consciousness* which influences the whole (4) *mind-body*, whose (5) *six sense-organs* allow (6) *contact* between each organ and its sense-object, giving rise to (7) *sensation* which leads to (8) *craving* for that sensation. Craving causes (9) *grasping* at future experiences which leads to (10) *becoming* or attachment to life in general leading to further (11) *birth* and thus (12) the *old age and death and the suffering* associated with them.

These twelve factors can be understood in different ways, but the main point remains the same. In response to the problem of how rebirth can occur without a permanent soul or self that is reborn, Buddhism explains rebirth as a series of impersonal processes which occur without any permanent self that is doing or experiencing them. In one Pali sutra, a monk asks the Buddha to whom belong, and for whom occur, the phenomena described in *pratitya-samutpada*. The Buddha rejects that question as misguided; from each factor as its preconditions arises another factor; that's all. Our *dukkha* "suffering" occurs without there being any self which causes or experiences the *dukkha*. The karmic results of action are experienced without there being any unchanging self which created the karma or any self which receives its fruit, although there is a causal connection between the action and its result.

Pratitya-samutpada was taught by the Buddha, yet some of its implications were not emphasized until the development of Mahayana. This was part of a philosophical self-deconstruction of the Buddhist teachings so influential that it has continued to reverberate through all subsequent Buddhist thought. The most important statement of this Madhyamika approach is in the *Mulamadhyamikakarika* of Nagarjuna, who is believed to have lived in the second century A.D.

The first verse of the *Mulamadhyamikakarika* proclaims its thoroughgoing critique of *self-existence*: "No things whatsoever exist, at any time or place, having risen by themselves, from another, from both or without cause." Nagarjuna's argument brings out more fully the implications of *pratitya-samutpada*, showing that dependent-origination should rather be understood as "non-dependent non-origination." *Pratitya-samutpada* does not teach a causal relation between entities, because the fact that these twelve factors are mutually dependent means that they are not really discrete entities; none could occur without the conditioning of all the other factors. In other words, none of its twelve phenomena—which are said to encompass everything—self-exists, because each is necessarily infected with the traces of all the others. That none is self-existing is the meaning of the most important Mahayana term *sunya*, which is usually translated as "empty." All things are "empty," because none has any essence or being of its own, everything being dependent on everything else.

However, that type of logic and epistemological analysis was less appealing to Chinese Buddhists, who preferred a more metaphorical way to express the interconditionality of all phenomena: the analogy of Indra's net described in the *Avatamsaka Sutra* and developed in the Hua-yen (*Kegon*) school of Mahayana.

Far away in the heavenly abode of the great god Indra, there is a wonderful net that has been hung by some cunning artificer in such a manner that it stretches out infinitely in all directions. In accordance with the extravagant tastes of deities, the artificer has hung a single glittering jewel in each "eye" of the net, and since the net itself is infinite in all dimensions, the jewels are infinite in number. . . . If we now arbitrarily select one of these jewels for inspection and look closely at it, we will discover that in its polished surface there are reflected all the other jewels in the net, infinite in number. Not only that, but each of the jewels reflected in this one jewel is also reflecting all the other jewels, so that there is an infinite reflecting process occurring. . . . [I]t symbolizes a cosmos in which there is an infinitely repeated interrelationship among all the members of the cosmos. This relationship is said to be one of simultaneous mutual identity and mutual inter-causality.[16]

Every "individual" is at the same time the effect of the whole and the cause of the whole, the totality being a vast, infinite body of members each sustaining and defining all the others. "The cosmos is, in short, a self-creating, self-maintaining, and self-defining organism." One of the most important consequences of this (also important for Taoism, and as we shall see, deep ecology) is that such a world is non-teleological: "There is no theory of a beginning time, no concept of a creator, no question of the purpose of it all. The universe is taken as a given." In such a universe, human beings cannot be considered the crown of creation, because it has no hierarchy: "There is no center, or, perhaps if there is one, it is every-where."[17]

This "mutual identity and inter-causality" of everything means that within this page you are now reading is nothing less than the entire universe. The Vietnamese Zen teacher (and poet) Thich Nhat Hanh makes this point best:

If you are a poet, you will see clearly that there is a cloud floating in this sheet of paper. Without a cloud, there will be no rain; without rain, the trees cannot grow, and without trees we cannot make paper. The cloud is essential for the paper to exist. If the cloud is not here, the sheet of paper cannot be here either. . . . If we look into this sheet of paper even more deeply, we can see the sunshine in it. If the sunshine is not there, the tree cannot grow. In fact, nothing can grow. Even we cannot grow without sunshine. And so, we know that the sunshine is also in this sheet of paper. The paper and the sunshine inter-are. And if we continue to look, we can see the logger who cut the tree and brought it to the mill to be transformed into paper. And we see the wheat. We know that the logger cannot exist without his daily bread, and therefore the wheat that became his bread is also in this sheet of paper. And the logger's father and mother are in it too. . . . You cannot point out one thing that is not here—time, space, the earth, the rain, the minerals in the soil, the sunshine, the cloud, the river, the heat. Everything co-exists with this sheet of paper. . . . As thin as this sheet of paper is, it contains everything in the universe in it.[18]

Again, Thich Nhat Hanh is not referring to our interdependence, for that would presuppose the existence of separate things which are related to-gether. Instead, everywhere there are only traces of everything else and those traces are traces of traces.

What do these abstract concepts mean for the way we live our lives? How does one actually realize and embody such interpenetration? D. T. Suzuki described Hua-yen as the philosophy of Zen, and Zen as the practice of Hua-yen. In a famous passage in his own *Shobogenzo*, the thirteenth century Japanese Zen Master Dogen sums up the process of Zen meditation as follows:

To study the Buddha Way is to study the self. To study the self is to forget the self. To forget the self is to be actualized by myriad things. When actualized by myriad things, your body and mind as well as the bodies and minds of others drop away. No trace of realization remains, and this no-trace continues endlessly.[19]

"Forgetting" ourselves is how we jewels in Indra's Net lose our sense of separation and realize that we are the net. Meditation is learning to forget the sense of self, which happens when I become absorbed into my meditation-exercise. Insofar as the sense of self is a result of consciousness reflecting back upon itself in order to grasp itself, such meditation practice makes sense as an exercise in de-reflection. Enlightenment occurs in Buddhism when the usually-automatized reflexivity of consciousness ceases, which is experienced as a letting go and falling into the void. "Men are afraid to forget their minds, fearing to fall through the Void with nothing to stay their fall. They do not know that the Void is not really void, but the realm of the real Dharma."[20] When consciousness stops trying to catch its own tail, I become no-thing, and discover that I am the world—or more precisely, that instead of being a subjective consciousness confronting it as an object, I am a manifestation of the world, interpenetrating it and interpenetrated by it. It is when I no longer strive to make myself real through things, that I find myself "actualized" by them, as Dogen puts it. Notice, however, what this does not mean. Such a realization does not involve a monistic dissolution of the self into Indra's Net nor a transcendence of the net. The interpenetration of all the jewels in the Net is not *sub specie aeternitas*, for there is no such Archimedean master-perspective. One is non-dual with the Net only by virtue of one's position within the Net. We can appreciate different perspectives, but there is no perspectiveless perspective. We are actualized by the myriad things, not something that transcends them; what unifies the whole Net is the web of interpenetrating traces that constitutes each of the myriad jewels. As a modern Zen master expresses it, with enlightenment "each thing just as it is takes on an entirely new significance or worth. Miraculously, everything is radically transformed though remaining just as it is."[21] In an earlier passage of the same *Shobogenzo* fascicle, Dogen emphasizes that this experience is not an expansion of ego-self but its disappearance: "To carry yourself forward and experience myriad things is delusion. That myriad things come forth and experience themselves is awakening."[22] Instead of incorporating the world into myself, self-forgetting allows the things of the world to "incorporate" me, in the sense that there is no self-existing me apart from the web of interpenetrating traces.

We seem to have drifted far from ethics; but the Buddhist approach to morality follows directly from this type of nondualistic identity with Indra's Net. When I discover that I *am* you, the trace of your traces, the ethical problem of how to relate to you is transformed. Loss of self-preoccupation entails the ability to respond to others without an ulterior motive that needs to gain something, material or symbolic, from that encounter. Of course, the danger of abuse remains, if my nondual experience is not deep enough to root out those dualistic tendencies that incline me to manipulate others. As long as there is sense of self, therefore, there will be need to inculcate morality, just as infants need training wheels on their bicycles. In Buddhism, however, ethical principles approximate the way of relating to others that nondual experience reveals; as in Christianity, I should love my neighbor as myself—in this case because the neighbor *is* myself. If we have developed to the degree that we spontaneously experience ourselves as one with others, we follow the precepts and endeavor to act as if we did feel at one. We have already noticed that, in contrast to the "Thou shalt not—or else!" of Mosaic law, the Buddhist precepts are undertakings: projects or paths one chooses to follow. These precepts are eventually realized not to rest on any objectively-binding moral principle. In my Zen school of *koan* practice, the last ten *koans* examine the ten Mahayana precepts from the enlightened point of view, to clarify what has become apparent: the precepts too are spiritual training wheels. There are no objective limitations on our freedom—except the dualistic delusions that incline us to abuse that freedom in the first place.

Such freedom is realized only when I realize my place in Indra's Net, which also entails my dependence upon all things. Goethe saw the paradox: you have only to consider yourself free to feel yourself bound, and you have only to consider yourself bound to feel free. We understand freedom as self-determination, that is, determination by one's *self*. But if there is no self, freedom needs to be understood differently. Why have questions of free will and liberty been so central in the Western tradition, to the extent that the pursuit of freedom might be considered its dominant myth? Freedom is the crucial issue for an ego-self *because it understands its basic problem as lack of autonomy*. So the origins of Western civilization are traced back to the Greek "emancipation" of reason from myth. Since the Renaissance, there has been a progressive emphasis, first on religious freedom (the Reformation), then political freedom (the English, American, French revolutions), followed by economic freedom (the class struggle), racial and colonial freedom, and most recently sexual and psychological freedom (psychotherapy, feminism, gay rights, etc.). Each of these struggles has been pursued with a religious fervor, for what is ultimately at stake in all of them is the right of the self to determine itself. The sad fact is that it is much easier to fight for freedom than to live freely. Absolute freedom for an ego-self is impossible, for our lack of self-existence ensures that we never experience ourselves as free enough: something is always felt to constrain us. As important as it is, the myth of freedom has been correlative to the project of the self-grounding ego-self, which seeks to eliminate all the ties that limit it so it can be truly self-determined. What does the search for freedom mean if self-groundedness is not possible? When even the most absolute freedom does not end *dukkha* but usually aggravates it (e.g., the last years of Howard Hughes), our struggle for freedom can be fulfilled only by transforming into a different quest. Goethe's statement implies that the greatest freedom comes from losing self-preoccupation and assuming responsibility for all things: not just for our family or our nation, but for the whole of Indra's Net. Present social and environmental conditions increasingly make such a commitment necessary.

For Buddhism such response-ability is not the means to salvation but natural to the expression of genuine enlightenment. Hee-Jin Kim explains Dogen's view of the Buddhist precepts as nothing other than *tathata* "thusness":

> *not-to-commit-any-evil* is neither the heteronomous "Thou shalt not" nor the autonomous "I will not," but is *non-contrivance*. . . . When morality becomes effortless, purposeless, and playful, it becomes a non-moral morality which is the culmination of Zen practice of the Way in which morality, art, and play merge together. When ought becomes *is* in the transparency of thusness, only then do we come to the highest morality.[23]

This is what might be called the "non-moral morality" of the *bodhisattva*, who having nothing to gain or lose him/herself—because he/she has no self—is devoted to the welfare of others. Contrary to popular Buddhist belief, this is not a personal sacrifice. The *bodhisattva* knows that no one is fully saved until everyone is saved; when I am the universe, to help others is to help myself. To become enlightened is to forget one's own suffering only to wake up at one with a world of suffering. This experience is not sympathy or empathy but compassion, literally "suffering with." What will the meaning of life become for such a person, freed from narcissistic self-preoccupation? What will that non-dual freedom, which has nothing to gain or to lose, choose to do? The career of the *bodhisattva* is helping others: not because one ought to, for traditionally the *bodhisattva* is not bound by dogma or morality, but because one is in the situation, and through oneself that situation draws forth a response to meet its needs.

What are the ecological implications of this approach? The first precept enjoins us not to kill any sentient being; the *bodhisattva* vows to help all beings become happy and realize their Buddha nature. As in Taoism, this denies the importance of the distinction we usually make between ourselves and other living beings. Such an attitude developed quite early in Buddhism, as in the popular *Jataka* "birth stories" which describe the earlier lives of the Buddha before he became the Buddha. Many *Jataka* passages celebrate the beauties of nature: forests, rivers and lakes, and most of all the wild creatures who are usually the protagonists of the stories. In many of the best-known stories the future Buddha sacrifices himself for "lower animals:" for example, offering his body to help a weak tigress feed her hungry cubs. In this fashion the *Jatakas* view the world non-dualistically as a vast field of spiritual effort in which no life-form, no matter how insignificant it seems to be, is outside the path. All beings are potential Buddhas and *bodhisattvas*. Each is able to feel compassion for the sufferings of others and act selflessly to ease the pain of all beings. The *Jatakas* also remind us that everything is food for something else, part of an all-encompassing food chain which does not end with humans.

Nor is this compassion limited to animals. The Buddha is believed to have experienced his great enlightenment under a *bodhi* (pipal) tree, and to have spent his first week after that contemplating this sheltering tree. Many passages in the Pali scriptures contain expressions of the Buddha's gratitude for trees and other plants. In one sutra, the spirit of a tree appears to the Buddha in a dream and complains that it had been chopped down by a monk. The next morning, the Buddha gathers the monks together and prohibits them from cutting down trees, for they too have sensate existence.

DEEP ECOLOGY

> The Western version of mystical awareness, our version of Buddhism or Taoism, will be ecological awareness.
>
> Fritjof Capra[24]

What has become known as deep ecology developed out of a critique of reformist environmentalism, which attempts to mitigate some of the worst forms of pollution, wildlife destruction, and short-sighted development schemes. The shortcomings of this approach, working within the framework of conventional political processes, soon became evident: such environmentalism tends to become technical and oriented to short-term public policy issues like resource allocation, without questioning more basic assumptions about the value of economic growth and development.

One of the earliest and best-known examples of a transformation to a deeper ecological approach was the naturalist Aldo Leopold, who in the 1920s and 1930s underwent a dramatic conversion from a "stewardship" resources-management mentality to what he termed an "ecological conscience." His new understanding was presented in *A Sand County Almanac* (1949), which argued for "biocentric equality" because "we are only fellow-voyagers with other creatures in the odyssey of evolution." To adopt an ecological conscience "changes the role of *Homo sapiens* from conqueror of the land-community to plain member and citizen of it." Leopold claimed that "the biotic mechanism is so complex that its working may never be fully understood," stressing the essential mysteriousness of life processes in a way that undercuts the possibility of its successful domination and control by humans. He went on to formulate an egalitarian "land ethic": "A thing is right when it tends to preserve the integrity, stability, and beauty of the biotic community. It is wrong when it tends otherwise."[25]

Leopold's subversive ideas were not appreciated for a generation, because they were too radical; like Taoism and Buddhism, they challenge some of our most deeply-rooted assumptions about the natural world, human beings, and the relationships between them. There are different ways to formulate these assumptions, of course, but they have been summarized into four basic propositions:

1. People are fundamentally different from all other creatures on Earth, over which they have dominion (defined as domination).
2. People are masters of their own destiny; they can choose their goals and learn to do whatever is necessary to achieve them.
3. The world is vast, and thus provides unlimited opportunities for humans.
4. The history of humanity is one of progress; for every problem there is a solution, and thus progress need never cease.[26]

According to this anthropocentric worldview (which can no longer be considered merely Western, since it has spread around the globe), the Earth is primarily if not exclusively a collection of natural resources waiting to be exploited. For those resources which are not infinite, our technology can provide substitutes. Human beings dominate nature because we are superior to the rest of nature. Other beliefs tend to be associated with the above assumptions; for example, the belief that the goal of life is comfort and convenience, and faith in technology and scientific progress. Historically, this set of values has not been concerned about the quality of the natural environment. The emphasis has been on individualism, with little awareness of the value of the human community, much less the biotic "land community" that Leopold described. The overriding value has been linking science and technology to exploit some aspect of nature—energy, minerals, forests, etc.—to serve the growing economy.[27]

This worldview remains dominant in its global reach, yet not unchallenged. Two important resources outside the Western tradition have already been discussed in the previous sections of this chapter. There have also been strong minority strands within the West: literary traditions such as romanticism and pastoralism; alternative Christian views of nature like that of St. Francis of Assisi; the lifestyles of "primal peoples" such as Native Americans; and today, less dualistic scientific models such as quantum mechanics and, of course, ecological biology itself. Within Western philosophy, two figures have been particularly important for those who want to challenge anthropocentrism (although both are controversial): Baruch Spinoza (1632–1677) and Martin Heidegger (1889–1976). It is noteworthy that, like Taoism and Buddhism, both philosophers deny the self-existence of anything, including us. For Spinoza, all beings are equal as manifestations of the one Substance, which for him has two modes: God and Nature. Although there are some passages in Spinoza's *Ethics* which state that we can treat other species as we like, the Norwegian philosopher Arne Naess has pointed out that this is inconsistent with the implications of his metaphysics.

[For Spinoza] all particular things are expressions of God; through all of them God acts. There is no hierarchy. There is no purpose, no final causes such that one can say that the "lower" exist for the sake of the "higher." There is an ontological democracy or equalitarianism which, incidentally, greatly offended his contemporaries, but of which ecology makes us more tolerant today.[28]

More recently, Martin Heidegger has made an influential critique of the Western philosophical tradition since Plato. In his view, its humanistic approach is responsible for the present technocratic mentality that espouses domination over nature. For Heidegger, the essence of technology is found in its tendency to perceive all beings as objective, quantifiable, and disposable raw material which is valued only insofar as it enhances our power. This understanding is both the culmination of Western civilization and the triumph of nihilism. In response, Heidegger offers a "new way of thinking" in which we dwell in the world with other beings, not as their master but by letting beings be so they can display themselves in all their glory.[29]

There are obvious similarities between Spinoza and Hua-yen Buddhism, and between Heidegger and Taoism, but before addressing them it will be helpful to generalize the argument by looking at what Warwick Fox, an Australian deep ecologist, considers its "central intuition": "It is the idea that we can make no firm ontological divide in the field of existence: That there is no bifurcation in reality between the human and the non-human realms."[30]

As an ontological claim, this denial of a bifurcation between the human and nonhuman realms is based on more than intuition; it follows from the essential ecological insight into the interrelatedness of everything. As John Muir said, when we try to pick out anything by itself, we find it hitched to everything else in the universe. That applies to us as much as to this sheet of paper that you are reading now. Yet there is still something lacking in this way of expressing it:

To the Western mind, *interrelatedness* implies a causal connectedness. Things are interrelated if a change in one affects the other. . . . But what is actually involved is a genuine intermingling of parts of the ecosystem. There are no discrete entities.[31]

Nagarjuna could not have put it better, for this is precisely his point: the doctrine of *pratitya-samutpada* "interdependent origination" leads us to the same conclusion. Thus Buddhism and ecology follow the same development. We usually begin with an understanding of the world as a collection of discrete beings, the most important being *us*. (Buddhism begins with the individual ego-self, ecology the collective "wego-self" that is *Homo sapiens*.) Buddhist teachings and ecological science lead to the realization that beings are not discrete; all our experience and all life-forms are inter-related; to isolate anything is to destroy it. Each living being is a dissipative structure, (i.e., does not endure in and of itself, but only due to a continual flow of energy into the system). Yet even this insight is incomplete, because if every*thing* is interrelated then there are no discrete things to be related-together. We end up with . . . Indra's infinite and interpenetrating Net, where each particular mirror is nothing other than a reflection of all the other mirrors which constitute the entire net: that is, each particular "thing" is what the whole universe is doing at this place and time.

However, what is most distinctive about deep ecology is the axiological corollary that it seems to derive from the above. This has been expressed most famously in the first (and most important) of the eight principles of the Deep Ecology Platform, initially formulated by Naess and George Sessions in 1984: "The well-being and flourishing of human and nonhuman Life on Earth have values in themselves. These values are independent of the usefulness of the nonhuman world for human purposes." Naess has developed this basic perspective into two "ultimate norms," i.e., ethical principles which in his opinion cannot be proven yet may be intuited. The first is *self-realization*, which goes beyond the self defined as an isolated ego striving for sense-gratification or for its own individual salvation. According to Naess, we must stop seeing ourselves as competing egos and learn to identify not only with other humans but with other species and even inanimate objects in the non-human world. The second ultimate norm is *biocentric equality*: all things in the biosphere have an equal right to live and blossom and to reach their own individual forms of unfolding and self-realization within the larger self-realization. This basic intuition is that all organisms and entities in the ecosphere, as parts of the interrelated whole, are equal in intrinsic worth.[32]

Both of these norms need to be examined, but first a clarification is necessary. Naess has always been careful to distinguish the Deep Ecology Platform from his own philosophy, which he calls Ecosophy. This is because he believes the Deep Ecology Platform can be logically derived from various, even incompatible, religious and philosophical premises.[33] It would be a mistake, therefore, to identify Naess's two norms as canonical for deep ecology, although some other deep ecologists overlook the distinction. This is particularly important for self-realization and identification, since some writers have elaborated Naess's concepts in ways that critics have shown to be problematic.

The biggest controversy has been over identification with the nonhuman world. Naess emphasizes this, but what does it mean? How can one identify with other species? Perhaps his best explanation is in his paper "Identification as a Source of Deep Ecological Attitudes":

There is a process of ever-widening identification and ever-narrowing alienation which widens the self. The self is as comprehensive as the totality of our identifications. . . . Identification is a spontaneous, non-rational, but not irrational, process through which the interests of another being are reacted to as our own interest or interests.[34]

Since this is still vague, it is not surprising that critics, especially eco-feminists, have identified problems with this approach. In an extended critique, Val Plumwood distinguishes three different accounts of the self in her reading of self-realization through identification: indistinguishability, which denies boundaries in the field of existence; the expansion of the self, which is an enlargement and extension of the ego-self; and transcendence of the self, which universalizes in a way that devalues personal relationships in favor of an abstractly conceived whole. All of these, she argues, involve an uncritical acceptance of rationalist and masculinist assumptions.[35]

Whether or not these criticisms apply to some other deep ecologists,[36] Naess's own writings reveal a sensitivity to precisely these problems. His very first paper on deep ecology was careful to characterize it in relational terms: "Rejection of the human-in-environment image in favour of the relational, total-field image. Organisms as knots in the biospherical net or field of intrinsic relations."[37] His most important book, *Ecology, Community, and Lifestyle*, points out that to see ourselves as intimately connected with nature is "a difficult ridge to walk: To the left we have the ocean of organic and mystic views, to the right the abyss of atomic individualism." At any level of realization of potentials, individual egos "do not dissolve like individual drops in the ocean," although "the individual is not, and will not be, isolatable."[38] In an unpublished essay on "Gestalt Thinking and Buddhism," Naess prefers the Buddhist *anatmavada* (no-self doctrine) to Hindu *atman*-absolutism because he stresses process rather than a Vedantic union with a transcendent Absolute.[39] In an interview, Naess has described the starting-point of his anti-Cartesian attitude as the desire "to overcome the entire subject-object cleavage as an axiom of modern philosophy. . . . It is as if I want to disappear." What is the way to do this? "To enmesh yourself in what you are doing, what you experience, in such a way that the relation to your ego disappears, and the Self is expanded into the World."[40] The similarity between this and Zen practice is as striking as the similarity between Naess's use of gestalt internal-relations and what Mahayana says about interpenetration. For Naess as with Indra's Net, the way for the self to realize that it is not separate from the world is for the ego-self to forget itself and "disappear." Then instead of the world as a collection of discrete objects confronting me, my true self is a vast web of traces and traces of traces.

This meets the feminist critique; such a self is not indistinguishable from the world in the way that each spoonful of porridge is indistinguishable from the next, nor is it the result of the ego-self expanding to incorporate the world. Instead of transcending personal relationships, such a loss of self-preoccupation can only deepen them, as part of one's involvement in the world generally.

To understand such a world, the static notion of entity must be replaced with something more dynamic. When we let go of our usual entity-way of looking at a collection of self-existing things, we end up with Buddhist insights about natural processes and events; for Buddhism too emphasises the impermanence of things. To realize this is to see that a flower is not an entity, it is the beautiful sexual gesture of a plant. Then Naess's second ultimate norm, that "all organisms and entities in the ecosphere are equal in intrinsic worth," may be better expressed as: every event is equal in intrinsic value to every other event.

This seems innocuous enough, yet it has extraordinary "moral" implications. Earlier we saw that the Hua-yen concept of Indra's Net is non-teleological and non-hierarchical: "There is no theory of a beginning time, no concept of a creator, no question of the purpose of it all." Human beings cannot be the crown of creation, because "there is no center, or, perhaps if there is one, it is everywhere."[41] We have also noticed that Arne Naess, in arguing for deep ecology, has derived the same insight from Spinoza's metaphysics: "There is no hierarchy. There is no purpose, no final causes such that one can say that the 'lower' exist for the sake of the 'higher.' There is an ontological democracy or equalitarianism." Now that entity-language has been translated into event-language, how shall we understand this? There is a famous Zen story about a sermon by Sakyamuni Buddha, when he said nothing but just twirled a flower in his hand. No one understood this except Mahakasyapa. Yet what did he understand? Just "this"! The entire universe exists just for the sake of this particular "flower" to bloom—and for the sake of "me" to appreciate it. Or, as deep ecologists might prefer to put it, the whole biosphere exists only for this oak tree to grow, for this river to flow, for this whale to spout.

Deep ecologists have elaborated on the meaning of "intrinsic worth" or "inherent value": "The presence of inherent value in a natural object is independent of any awareness, interest, or appreciation of it by a conscious being."[42] This is diametrically opposed to our usual understanding of nature, but it is deeply congruent with Taoism and Heidegger's work, both of which emphasize "letting things be" in order for them to flourish; not for our sake, and not even for their own sakes, but for no sake at all—because questions of utility and justification no longer apply. For Heidegger, "dwelling is not primarily inhabiting, but taking care of and creating that space within which something comes into its own and flourishes."[43] The teleological question "what for?" arises out of the anthropocentric attitude which perceives all beings as quantifiable and disposable raw material, and which values beings only insofar as they are good for something—in effect, good for our own purposes. "Letting things be" challenges that basic principle of our technological and consumerist society, but it also subverts our notion of ego-self. This brings us back to again the first "ultimate norm" that Naess derives from the non-duality between the human and non-human realms: self-realization, which includes learning to identify with the whole of the biosphere. To admit that natural objects (natural events) have an inherent value independent of any awareness or appreciation by other beings is to question our commonsense dualism between the conscious self and the objective world.

If I am "in here" (behind the eyes and inside the ears, as it were) and the world is "out there," the alienation between us makes value subjective: it can only be a function of my desires and my projects. Then to deny such an anthropocentric understanding of value, as deep ecology does, also leads us to question the dualism between subject and object. We have already noticed how Taoism and Buddhism deny that dualism. For Taoism all the ten thousand things, including us, are mere "straw-dogs" in themselves, because they have no reality apart from being manifestations of the Tao. Zen master Dogen realized that his mind was "nothing other than mountains and rivers and the great wide earth, the sun and the moon and the stars." Perhaps it is inevitable, although nonetheless a shock, that some deep ecologists have arrived at the same conclusion:

When humans investigate and see through their layers of anthropocentric self-cherishing, a most profound change in consciousness begins to take place.

Alienation subsides. The human is no longer an outsider, apart. Your humanness is then recognized as being merely the most recent stage of your existence . . . you start to get in touch with yourself as mammal, as vertebrate, as a species only recently emerged from the rain forest. As the fog of amnesia disperses, there is a transformation in your relationship to other species, and in your commitment to them. . . . "I am protecting the rain forest" develops to "I am part of the rain forest protecting myself. I am that part of the rain forest recently emerged into thinking."[44]

We are back within Indra's Net: "I am that part of Indra's Net recently emerged into thinking." What began as a scientific claim, about the ecological inter-relatedness of species, has developed here into a religious claim: not just any religious claim, but the fundamental realization of Taoism and Buddhism.

Yet it is not wolves or whales or trees but humans who make such a claim and endeavor to realize it. This raises a question about Fox's "central intuition" that there is no real bifurcation between the human and nonhuman realms, for there does seem to be an important difference: we humans are the only dissipative structures who can realize that we are not separate from Indra's Net: that moreover we are not parts of the Net but the whole of the Net, come to consciousness at this particular place and time. Or is it that we are the sole species which needs to pursue self-realization, because the sole species whose self-consciousness alienates it in the first place? The etymology usually given for the English word *religion* traces it back to the Latin *re + ligio* "to bind back together."

Homo sapiens seems to be the only animal that needs religion, because it is the only one deluded by an ego-self that needs to be reunified with the world. So we can understand why Fritjof Capra thinks that the Western version of Taoism and Buddhism will be ecological awareness: because deep ecology has also come to realize the importance of solving the basically religious issue of the alienation between ourselves and the world we find ourselves "in." The individual ego-self and the species "wego-self" turn out to be different versions of the same problem, which can be resolved only by realizing that the duality between ourselves and the natural world is delusive. The environmental catastrophes which are occurring more and more often make it evident that such a transformation is necessary if we—not only humans, but the rich diversity that constitutes the biosphere—are to survive and thrive through the next century.[45]

NOTES

This chapter originally appeared in *Worldviews: Environment, Culture, Religion* 1 (1997): 249–273. © 1997 The White Horse Press, Cambridge, UK. Reproduced with permission.

1. Quoted in Fox 1990, p. 106.
2. Zimmerman 1983, p. 112.
3. In Devall and Sessions 1985, p. 66.
4. *Chuang-tzu*, with Kuo Hsiang's commentary, trans. Fung Yu-lan (New York: Gordon Press, 1975), pp. 34, 46.
5. As quoted in deBary 1964, p. 69; my italics.
6. *Pancapadika* VI. 285.
7. For such an analysis, see Loy 1988, pp. 112–124.
8. *Chuang-tzu*, op. cit., p. 53.
9. Quoted in Yalom 1980, p. 469.
10. Quoted in Chung-yuan Chang 1971, p. 22. A Vedantic equivalent is found in the *Bhagavad-gita*: "He who in action sees inaction and action in inaction—he is wise among men. . . . Having abandoned attachment to the fruit of works, ever content without any kind of dependence, he does nothing though he is ever engaged in work" (IV.18, 20).
11. Huxley 1969.
12. Schumacher 1975, p. 30. See also Loy 1994.
13. As quoted in Kapleau 1965, p. 205. The original reference is from the *Sokushin-zebutsu* fascicle of Dogen's *Shobogenzo*.

14. The present Dalai Lama has further simplified this: "All of Buddhism can be summed up in two sentences: If you have the ability, then help others. If not, at least do not harm them."

15. *Bodhicaryavatara* VIII. 120.

16. Cook 1977, p. 2.

17. Ibid.

18. Thich Nhat Hanh, 1988, pp. 3–5.

19. *Genjo-koan*, trans. Dan Welch and Kazuaki Tanahashi, in Tanahashi 1985, p. 70.

20. Bloefeld 1958, p. 41.

21. Yasutani's "Commentary on Mu," in Kapleau 1965, p. 80.

22. "Genjo-koan," p. 69.

23. Kim 1975, p. 294; Kim's italics.

24. Quoted in Fox 1984.

25. Leopold 1968.

26. Catton and Dunlap 1980.

27. Devall and Sessions 1985, p. 44.

28. Naess 1977. Naess has also written on the relation between Spinoza and Mahayana Buddhism; for example, Naess 1978.

29. Michael Zimmerman, who was among the first to point out the environmental relevance of Heidegger's critique of technology (see note 2 above), has since argued that Heidegger's version of anti-modernism is still anthropocentric and incompatible with deep ecology in several important respects. See Zimmerman 1994, especially chs. 1 and 3.

30. Quoted in Devall and Sessions 1985, p. 66.

31. Evernden 1978. Scientific ecology has recently become more reductive, with ecosystem paradigms challenged by more individualistic models emphasising flux and perturbation over harmony and balance. This does not contradict the type of interpenetration that Hua-yen emphasizes, which also denies stability and emphasizes flux.

32. Devall and Sessions 1985, pp. 66–67.

33. Naess has clarified this distinction with an "apron diagram" which distinguishes level 1 (ultimate premises) from level 2 (platform principles), level 3 (general lifestyle/policy views) and level 4 (practical and concrete decisions). This diagram is reproduced in Drengson and Inoue 1995, pp. 11–12.

34. In Tobias 1985, p. 261.

35. Plumwood 1993, pp. 176 ff.

36. Plumwood's argument seems more applicable to, e.g., Warwick Fox, who presents a "cosmological" interpretation of identification (Fox 1990).

37. "The Shallow and the Deep, Long-Range Ecology Movement: A Summary" (1973), reprinted in Drengson and Inoue 1995, p. 3; Naess's own italics.

38. Naess 1988, pp. 165, 195.

39. Cited in Ingvar Anda, "Arne Naess's Gestalt Ontology and Sunyata: a Comparative Analysis," unpublished.

40. In Rothenberg 1993, p. 76.

41. Cook 1977, p. 2.

42. Regan 1981, pp. 19–34.

43. Quoted in Tobias 1985, p. 250.

44. John Seed, "Anthropocentrism," in Tobias 1985, p. 243.

45. The revised version of this paper has benefited from comments by Clare Palmer, Ingvar Anda, and the anonymous reviewer for *Worldviews*.

REFERENCES

Bloefeld, John (trans.). 1958. *The Zen Teaching of Huang Po*. London: Buddhist Society.

Catton, William, Jr., and Riley Dunlap. 1980. "New Ecological Paradigm for Post-Exuberant Sociology." *American Behavioral Scientist* 24:15–48.

Chang, Chung-yuan (trans.). 1971. *Original Teachings of Ch'an Buddhism*. New York: Vintage.

Cook, Francis H. 1977. *Hua-yen Buddhism: The Jewel Net of Indra*. University Park, PA: The Pennsylvania State University Press.

deBary, Theodore (ed.). 1964. *Sources of Chinese Tradition*. New York: Columbia University Press.

Devall, Bill, and George Sessions. 1985. *Deep Ecology: Living as if Nature Mattered*. Salt Lake City: Peregrine Smith Books.

Drengson, Alan and Yuichi Inoue (eds.). 1995. *The Deep Ecology Movement: An Introductory Anthology*. Berkeley, CA: North Atlantic.

Evernden, Neil. 1978. "Beyond Ecology." *North American Review* 263: 16–20.

Fox, Warwick. 1984. "The Intuition of Deep Ecology." *The Ecologist*.

Fox, Warwick. 1990. *Toward a Transpersonal Ecology: Developing New Foundations for Environmentalism*. Boston: Shambhala.

Huxley, Aldous. 1969. *Eyeless in Gaza*. London: Chatto and Windus.

Kapleau, Philip (ed.). 1965. *The Three Pillars of Zen*. Tokyo: Weatherhill.

Kim, Hee-Jin. 1975. *Dogen Kigen—Mystical Realist*. Tucson: University of Arizona Press.

Leopold, Aldo. 1968. *A Sand County Almanac*. New York: Oxford University Press.

Loy, David. 1988. *Nonduality: A Study in Comparative Philosophy*. New Haven, CT: Yale University Press.

Loy, David. 1994. "Preparing for Something that Never Happens: the Means/Ends Problem in Modern Culture." *International Studies in Philosophy* 6(4).

Naess, Arne. 1977. *Ecology, Community, and Lifestyle, A Philosophical Approach*. Oslo: Oslo University Press.

Naess, Arne. 1978. "Through Spinoza to Mahayana Buddhism, or Through Mahayana Buddhism to Spinoza?" In Jon Wetlesen (ed.), *Spinoza's Philosophy of Man*. Oslo: Oslo University Press.

Naess, Arne. 1988. *Ecology, Community and Lifestyle*. Cambridge: Cambridge University Press.

Plumwood, Val. 1993. *Feminism and the Mastery of Nature*. London: Routledge.

Regan, Tom. 1981. "The Nature and Possibility of an Environmental Ethic." *Environmental Ethics* 3.

Rothenberg, David. 1993. *Is It Painful to Think? Conversations with Arne Naess*. Minneapolis: University of Minnesota Press.

Schumacher, E. F. 1975. *Small Is Beautiful*. New York: Harper and Row.

Spinoza, Benedict de. 1994. *Ethics and Other Works*. Edwin Curley, ed. and trans. Princeton, NJ: Princeton University Press.

Tanahashi, Kazuaki (ed.). 1985. *Moon in a Dewdrop: Writings of Zen Master Dogen*. San Francisco: North Point Press.

Thich Nhat Hanh. 1988. *The Heart of Understanding*. Berkeley, CA: Parallax Press.

Tobias, Michael (ed.). 1985. *Deep Ecology*. San Diego, CA: Avant.

Yalom, Irvin D. 1980. *Existential Psychotherapy*. New York: Basic Books.

Zimmerman, Michael. 1983. "Towards a Heideggerian Ethos for Radical Environmentalism." *Environmental Ethics 5*.

Zimmerman, Michael. 1994. *Contesting Earth's Future: Radical Ecology and Postmodernity*. Berkeley, CA: University of California Press.

6

Ethics for the Coming Century: A Buddhist Perspective

CARL B. BECKER

THE BASIS OF BUDDHIST ETHICS

Buddhism has often been criticized as a religion of passivity, withdrawal, or even world-denial. Indeed, there are periods and peoples for which this characterization aptly applies. But from its very inception, Buddhism is at root a highly practical and ethical philosophy. Let us consider (1) the principles and basis for Buddhist ethics; (2) examples of how these principles apply to contemporary ethical problems, and (3) the ways in which such teaching can be most effectively communicated. Throughout this discussion, we shall use Buddhism to refer not to a particular sect or group of believers, but to a philosophical attitude and way of looking at the world which can be equally well followed by people who do not think of themselves as Buddhists. Buddhism is chosen here because it exemplifies certain classical Asian ways of thinking with particular clarity and authority.

It is true that Gautama Siddhartha left his home and family in order to seek enlightenment. But Buddha's achievement of enlightenment marks the end of his withdrawal from the world, and the beginning of a 45-year-long career of commitment and teaching to relieve the suffering of humanity. Some tales relate that he was tempted to remain withdrawn from the world, and felt an internal struggle as to whether to involve or detach himself after his enlightenment. Surely every philosopher and religious person find times when a detached perspective on the world is needed, when the pettiness of worldly activity loses all appeal. But the Buddha returned from his meditations to found an ongoing community of believers which ultimately spread non-violently throughout half of the literate world. His "Middle Way" rejected both the self-immolating asceticism which would utterly reject the world, and the self-indulgent hedonism which would flounder in the world's delusions. This ethical worldview is more valuable than ever amid the problems that the world faces today.

The starting point, the root and core of Buddhism through all its historical and cultural manifestations, is the Four Noble Truths:

1. All is suffering (or "unsatisfactory"; Sanskrit: *dukkha*). "Birth is ill, decay is ill, sickness is ill, death is ill. To be conjoined with what one dislikes means suffering. To be disjoined from what one likes means suffering. Not to get what one wants also means suffering. . . ." (Conze 1959, p. 43)
2. The cause of suffering is desire.
3. The solution to suffering is control of desires.
4. This can be achieved through a moral life, the Eightfold Noble Path (right views, right intention, right speech, right action, right livelihood, right effort, right mindfulness, right meditation).

Some of these propositions may appear either counterintuitive or unduly pessimistic, especially in any translation away from their original Pali/Sanskrit nuances. A more careful reading shows them to be truths which hold deep hope for the possibilities of human improvement, which non-Buddhists as well as Buddhists can easily embrace. Let us therefore analyze them a little more deliberately.

1. To say that all is suffering or unsatisfactory is grounded on the recognition that all experiences and phenomena are *anicca*, impermanent; there are physico-temporal limits to all material things. This does not mean that there are not moments of pleasurable experience. It rather suggests that the more we become attached to any pleasurable experiences, the more we miss them when we can no longer experience them, whether they be food and drink, entertainment, or the company of friends. The Buddha is emphatic that this does not mean that we should not care for the body or value good friendships. Rather, a recognition of their impermanence makes them simultaneously dearer when we can experience them, and less missed after they are gone, for our minds were already prepared for that inevitability.

There have been cultures and philosophies which have believed in their own permanence, such as the Roman Empire and the Third Reich. Other societies with very small populations and very large lands for foraging have believed in an unlimited abundance of material resources. Today, however depressing, the truth of the limitation and impermanence of all physical phenomena and material resources is a scientifically demonstrable fact. No people, no country, no river or forest will live forever, and the earth's natural resources are rapidly approaching their final limits. A recognition of this fundamental limitation of time and matter constitutes the first enlightened awakening to the unsatisfactoriness of material existence; one does not need to be a Buddhist to admit this state of affairs.

2. Like most religious sages, the Buddha wrestled with the question of why humans must suffer. His conclusion places the responsibility not on some mythical ancestors who violated the will of heaven, nor on a capricious or wrathful creator, nor on a struggle between superhuman forces of good and evil, light and darkness. In the Buddhist view, such "answers" simply relegate the question of human suffering to the realm of the unanswerable. For any further inquiry into "How we can know that is the reason why people suffer?" is met only with statements of faith, not easily open to further discussion or vindication.

The Buddha's approach demonstrates a rational commitment to cause and effect. Not only the Buddha, but countless commentators in succeeding centuries have stressed that Buddhism is an intensely empirical philosophy, highly concerned with causality, rationality, and comprehension. In instances where we suffer from cold, hunger, or sickness, it is obvious that suffering is caused by our *desires* for heat, food, or health. The less obvious but critical corollary is that in our attempts to relieve our sufferings, we inevitably produce suffering of some other kind: generating heat and pollution to warm ourselves, killing plants and animals to feed ourselves and test our medications, or burdening others with taking care of us. The more that these causal webs of interconnectedness are realized, the more the two truths of suffering and of its causes become apparent.

3. The third noble truth (that the solution to suffering is the control of desires) again attests to both the rigorous rationality and positive hopefulness of the Buddhist attitude. The second truth (that desire causes suffering) does not imply or entail that destroying desires will destroy suffering, as some illogical people might conclude. For example, smoking causes cancer, and malnutrition causes blindness, but this does not entail that elimination of smoking will eliminate cancer, nor that elimination of malnutrition will eliminate blindness. So the third truth is importantly different and logically independent from the second.

The ability of humans to control their desires is emphatically affirmed in this statement. A more pessimistic Freudian or Darwinian view might say that humans are fundamentally ruled by their animal natures, that our drives for power, sex, satisfaction, and status, are beyond our control. If so, the world is doomed indeed. For the principles of competition and appropriation of resources which led to the evolution and ascent of humankind now threaten to destroy the entire planet through environmental degradation if not through thermonuclear accident. Only if humans can reverse their animal tendencies to fight and to appropriate resources can the present disastrous trends be reversed.

Fortunately, humans can control their desires. We learn to consume foods and excrete wastes not when we most desire to do so, but when it least inconveniences others. We learn to suppress anger, greed, conflict, and fear, and ultimately to overcome them by communication, reason, compromise, and equanimity. We learn to redirect our drives for power, sex, or physical pleasures into creative channels of sports, arts, and self-cultivation. That not enough humans have learned to control themselves is sadly evidenced by the continuity of war, crime, and suffering through the ages. That it is possible to do so is manifest in our daily lives, and fundamental to the Buddhist hope for the world.

   4. The moral life is exemplified by the Eightfold Noble Path, and also by the moral life of the Buddha himself. Unlike Judeo-Christian commandments, Kant's deontological duties, or the hedonistic calculus of the utilitarians, the Buddhist Way is neither a set of rules nor calculations, but rather an *attitude* of friendliness and compassion, humility and equanimity (deBary 1972, p. 32). It is consciously altruistic, as in the Buddha's words, "he who would care for me should care for the sick."

   The four cardinal vices in Buddhism are:

1. injury to life
2. taking what is not one's own
3. base sexual conduct
4. false speech

and there are also repeated injunctions against squandering wealth (deBary 1972, pp. 36, 40). These are not absolute commandments, but rather goals toward which all can strive. While Buddha advocated vegetarianism as an ideal, he accepted and ate meat that was given to him, when not specifically killed for his consumption. While condemning stealing, Buddhist communities inevitably use and pollute air, water, earth, and other resources, with an attitude of apologetic reverence. While the complete overcoming of sexual desire and of seeing people as sexual objects is held as an ideal, the importance of family life is strongly upheld. The Buddha admonishes businessmen to reinvest their profits into their business, in order to make money without hurting others (deBary 1972, p. 42). He advocates that the young should care for their elders, and masters should care for their workers—in other words, that those with means and responsibility should care for those who lack the means to face their various needs. Thus, the Buddhist attitude is less one of following a rule book than of maintaining "right mindfulness"—a consciousness of how one's actions affect others, and of how one's thoughts affect one's own psycho-spiritual progress.

   In overview, the essential truth of Buddhism is that inner peace and happiness depends not on external wealth or conditions, but on a state of mind, and that regardless of external conditions, a state of mind can be cultivated to maintain peace and inner happiness. At the same time, this does not mean that external conditions are ignored or forgotten. The last words of the Buddha: "All things must pass. Strive onward vigilantly!" are illustrative in this regard. The equanimity of enlightenment must be exemplified in one's life style and communicated to one's community in order to diminish the present and future suffering of sentient beings.

ETHICS FOR SURVIVAL ON AN ENDANGERED PLANET

Recognizing Interdependence, Impermanence, and Cause-and-Effect

The middle path is the only way in which our ecosystem can expect to avoid massive disturbances which will upset the balance of life on the planet. The Buddhist truth of the limitation and interdependence of all things is well illustrated in the cases of air, fire (energy), and earth (raw materials). Let us look at each of these examples in turn.

Air

Aside from the inert gas nitrogen, the atmosphere of our planet is composed primarily of oxygen and carbon-oxygen compounds. Animals' breathing and fuel combustion combine carbon with oxygen to deplete the oxygen supply and increase the amount of CO_2 in the air. On the other side, plants' respiration takes carbon from the CO_2 to leave pure oxygen (O_2) in the air. It is for this reason that the tropical rainforests are often called "the lungs of the earth."

The balance can be depicted as follows:

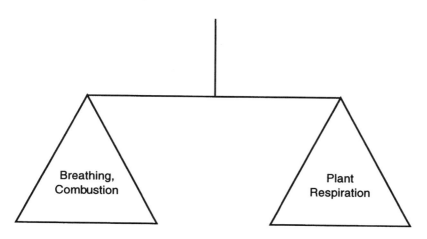

In pre-industrial ages, the amount of oxygen turned into CO_2 by animal breathing and fire (combustion) was less than the amount of CO_2 turned into oxygen by plant life all over the planet, so there was a surplus of oxygen in the atmosphere and of energy stored as carbon compounds in living and dead plant matter. In the past century, the sudden combustion of millions of years of fossil plant matter, the deforestation of vast areas of the world for fuel and lumber, and the rapid increase of both the human and livestock populations around the world have reversed that balance, so that every year now, more CO_2 is being poured into the atmosphere than the declining plant population can convert.

The reduction of oxygen and increase of airborne carbons have deleterious effects. Lack of oxygen impairs brain functions, and airborne carbons cause lung cancer. Both aggravate global warming, whereby rising oceans menace coastal populations, changing rainfall patterns aggravate desertification and deforestation, unprecedented windstorms demolish property, exploding insect populations ravage crops and spread epidemics, and temperature extremes disrupt the entire food chain.

It is therefore obvious that we need to increase the vegetated areas of the world and to decrease both human combustion of fossil fuels and the number of oxygen-consuming beings on the planet. (The problem of fossil fuels will be further discussed under "Energy" below.) It is easy to reduce the population of feed animals such as cattle, sheep, hogs, and chickens, and to increase the protein-production and vegetation of the world at the same time, by turning pasture and farmland now used only for animal fodder into fields of soybeans and other legumes. Beans produce far more protein per acre than does animal husbandry, and they have the added advantage of converting both CO_2 and NO_2 into oxygen and soil-enriching nitrogen and carbon compounds. Moreover, meat consumption has been clearly linked to cancers and heart diseases.

In short, a vegetarian or nearly vegetarian diet like that advocated by traditional Buddhists is not only supportive of individual human health, but is ultimately required for the balance of vegetation and perpetuation of the atmosphere itself. And the Buddhist principle of sexual self-control (in terms of family planning) is becoming increasingly necessary as the world population approaches the absolute limits of the world's food supply.

Fire (Energy)

Since long before the beginning of life on earth, the earth's energy has come from the sun. The sun is responsible for the energy of light radiation stored by plants, heat radiation stored by the oceans, and convection energy seen in the movement of winds and ocean currents. Additional sources of sustainable energy are indirectly dependent on the sun: winds caused by the earth's rotation, tides caused by the moon's gravity, thermal energy from the earth's magma, and water power caused by the evaporation and condensation of rainwater. Such sources of energy are sustainable in the sense that, like the sun, they are likely to continue for billions of years into the future.

On the other hand, there are exhaustible sources of energy. These consist of combustible fossil and present plant matter, and radioactive materials such as uranium. Once these sources of energy have released the energy stored within them, they can never again be returned to their original state. Disposal of their waste products, whether carboniferous or radioactive, poses permanent problems to our air, sea, and land. The heat they release into the air and water is difficult to recapture, and contributes to the global warming problems noted above. And they are strictly limited: once the oil, coal, and uranium of the earth's crust are gone, they are gone forever. There can be no doubt that humans need to turn from exhaustible energy consumption to sustainable energy generation. The question is only one: will we invest in the technology to generate sustainable energy in time to meet the need for it?

Two Buddhist principles hit directly at this issue: the principle of not taking what is not given, and the principle of limiting one's own desires. From a Buddhist viewpoint, what is always given is the sun's energy, light, and heat, and the rains and winds that it produces. If we learn to generate all our energy from the light, heat, rains, and winds that are given to us, then there will be neither undue polluting of the environment nor exhaustion of irreplaceable energy resources. If all our best efforts to produce energy from sustainable sources fail to produce enough for human needs (which is highly unlikely), then we can also learn to limit our desires to the amount of the available energy.

At present, annual world energy consumption is rising at an astronomical rate, because (1) the population of the world is increasing, and (2) the per capita energy consumption is increasing. Even if we are able to achieve the ideal of zero population growth (which requires the limiting of desires for sex and progeny), world energy consumption will continue to rise annually as long as humans continue to desire increasingly energy-consumptive life styles, from electric blankets to electric toothbrushes and can openers. Ultimately, the Buddhist principle of limiting one's own desires has to be applied not only to family planning, but to personal and family energy consumption. This need not be intrinscially difficult; it is largely a matter of coming to the realization that we can live quite healthy and happy lives without the vast majority of energy-consuming devices to which we have developed attachments.

Earth (Natural Resources)

As is true of the oxygen and fuel supplies of the earth, there are also definite limits to the minerals, carbons, and silicates from which we produce metal, plastic, and ceramic fibers and materials. There are two possible scenarios for the use of these limited resources: that of single use and waste disposal, or that of recycling. They might be diagrammed as follows:

One-way destructive consumption and waste production:

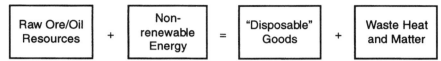

Cyclical recycling and re-use:

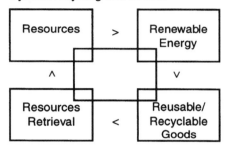

Primitive tribes of humans used slash-and-burn agriculture. They moved from forest to forest, burning the vegetation to provide space and ash fertilizer for their single crops. Then in a year or two, they deserted the now denuded and leached soil to burn another area of vegetation. As long as the population was very small compared to the vegetated land area, these people were unaware of the ecological problems they were causing. With the agricultural revolution, people learned that the only way to stably support larger populations was to continue reusing the same land, through crop rotation, fallow years, and returning wastes to the soil as fertilizer.

"Slash-and-burn" mining and manufacturing must also come to a similar realization. As long as the population using the minerals of the earth's crust is very small, the damage of one-time mining and waste disposal is not very visible. However, as the world population expands, and the majority of the world population wants to consume mineral, plastic, and ceramic products, there arises the dual problem of the exhaustion of unreplenishable resources and the disposal of huge quantities of waste. Just as we learned to give up slash-and-burn agriculture for cyclical land re-use, we must soon learn to give up the consumption and waste of resources for a more cyclical re-use of the minerals, polymers, and ceramics on our earth's limited crust. This, too, depends fundamentally on a Buddhist-type realization of limitation and interdependence, and on our limiting of our desires to the situation.

Another response needs to be in the way of education, especially in the areas of birth control and family planning. No matter how much each individual reduces his or her consumption of energy, as long as the world population continues to soar, the total energy consumption and pollution will continue to escalate geometrically. Traditional religions have often advocated large families, for having many children in an age of high mortality rates was necessary to ensure that the grandparents would be cared for in their old age. Moreover, each ethno-religious group felt that its own prosperity and power would be best served by having more numbers than the adjacent religious or ethnic group. Ironically, this led some religions to compete with their neighbors to have the most children.

Such thinking is tragically out-of-date, and needs to be repudiated by authorities at every level, not the least by Buddhists. Buddhists are fundamentally concerned with seeing humans as individuals and communities, not as numbers, looking at quality of life, not quantity. Political and environmental peace will never be achieved until stable populations are achieved throughout the world.

Changing Desires for Self into Compassion/Desires for All

The need for humans to come to peace with nature needs no underscoring. For thousands of years, the most densely populated societies on earth led lives well-balanced within the limits of their natural surroundings. They were largely vegetarian, used renewable energy sources, and their populations were kept in check by infanticide and by the limits of the food supply.

The advent of industrial capitalism and the technological revolution changed all that. Advances in industry and transportation required the import of non-renewable fossil fuels and the export of pollution across regional and national boundaries. The demand of the richer countries for lumber and other natural resources has led to the destruction of tropical rainforests in large portions of South America and Asia. Meanwhile, both the advanced countries and the increasingly populated areas of the world are increasing their demands for fuel, radiation-producing devices, and even fluorocarbons. This is depleting the world's oxygen and ozone supply, leading to catastrophic changes in climate and rises in cancer and other diseases.

These problems have long since passed a merely local or regional level. Japan's construction industry, for example, is deforesting the island of Sarawak, while its garbage is being shipped to Taiwan and other Southeast Asian locations where pollution controls are lax enough that massive poisons can still be released into the water and atmosphere. Numerous animal species, particularly the larger mammals such as bears, tigers, wolves, and whales, are on the verge of extinction forever.

There is already enough scrap metal, plastic, and fiber in many countries to serve for years without additional mining and lumbering. The linear view that things can be produced "from nothing" and then discarded "to return to nothing" obscures the fact that the ore that is once mined will never become ore again, and the poisons once released when a plastic is burned will never return to a plastic shape again. The mistaken materialist world-view must be replaced by the more enlightened cyclical understanding that all things are interdependent; that old cars, telephones, and batteries can be melted into new cars, telephones, and batteries. Industry will only be influenced to move in this direction when the voice of the consumer is felt, so to change the mind-set of the consumer about what is desirable to purchase is a fundamental mission of any environmentally-minded religious organization. At the same time, religious buildings and facilities can serve as recycling centers for paper, glass, metal, and plastic, with the proceeds going to further encourage environmental ethics.

The recognition that indeed the earth is fundamentally sacred is essential to all the major religions. Christians are developing the idea of "Steward-ship Ethics"; that humans need to care for the earth with which we have been "entrusted." Buddhists recognize the Buddha-nature in all things, and are consequently reluctant to take life needlessly. Taoism, Shinto, and a multitude of local religions in Asia are particularly attuned to the sacred-ness of nature and life. These religions can unite with Buddhists in opposing the thoughtless destruction of nature for the sake of greed or personal gain.

The Buddhist goal of "desirelessness" does not mean that Buddhists de-sire nothing. Obviously, they must have desires for enlightenment, equa-nimity, peace of mind, and compassion. The Eightfold Noble Path presupposes that Buddhists will desire to follow each of its steps, and the second step is explicitly "Right Intentions," which could be equally well translated as "Rightful Desires." The point is not that Buddhists may not desire anything, but that their desires must be in accord with the interde-pendent equanimity, peace of mind, and welfare of the whole, and not with self-serving greed or grasping materialism.

Modern capitalism glorifies personal property, evaluates people on their income and possessions, and encourages conspicuous consumption. In this sense, it is both the culprit behind the destruction and waste which we observed above, and the direct opposite of Buddhist ideals. Unless the cap-italist system is overhauled or redirected, motivation for environmental bal-ance will always be subordinate to motivation for personal aggrandizement, and a stable and ethical ecosystem will never be achieved. Changes of both economic structure and consumer attitude are required.

Ultimately, the economic structure must be changed to return the costs of recycling, replanting, and de-polluting to the manufacturer and con-sumer. This already happens in cases of things like water and paper, where the cost of purifying the water is passed on by the purification plant to the consumer, or the cost of replanting the paper company's forests is passed on to the paper buyer. However, it needs to become the rule throughout every phase of every industry. The costs of melting an old car into steel and plastic need to be included in the cost of a new car. The costs of recycling the billions of "disposable" cameras and food containers sold annually need to be incorporated into their prices. The costs of detoxifying toxic wastes need to be built into the prices of the chemicals which produce such wastes. Only when this level of realization and responsibility is achieved with regard to every good and service sold will ecological equilibrium be compatible with capitalism.

The other change needed is that of consumer attitude. Ultimately, peace with nature will not be achieved until all people become conscious of the effects of their actions. Each time I switch on an electrical device, or drive a vehicle rather than walking or bicycling, I am also warming the globe, polluting the air or sea, and depleting the world of already limited fuel. Each time I use synthetic rather than natural chemicals (such as detergents rather than soaps), I am disturbing a balance of nature for generations to come. Each time I choose to eat beef rather than beans, I am voting to deplete the oxygen as well as the supply of land usable for human sustenance.

Such consciousness does not require immediate abandonment of all powered appliances, vehicles, and animal proteins. It leads, however, to a reverence and conservationism like that of the persons who pray in their hearts, "Forgive me that I must take the life of this tree to preserve my own life. Let me revere this tree throughout all its future forms and incarnations, so that it shall not be said that I have wasted the life of an irreplaceable living being." Such an attitude is indeed the epitome of Buddhist humility, and a Buddhist-style ethical attitude can foster such a consciousness working toward the achievement of peace and balance of mankind and nature.

The point is not that Buddhists (and all humans) need to achieve utter desirelessness; Buddhism is not a philosophy of apathy. It is rather that desires for personal aggrandizement need to be changed into desires for the healthy continuity of the human community and indeed of the biosphere. It means replacing desires for the satiation of fleeting physical needs with desires for lasting spiritual and ethical satisfaction. It means finding deeper satisfaction in service to others and deeper enjoyment in responsibility for beauty than in self-serving consumption. This is neither idealistic nor difficult to attain. We are all familiar with the glow of satisfaction in having cleaned something which was foul or polluted, with the pleasure of seeing others enjoy healthy activity, with the inner joy of having done what needed doing to complete some project, with or without public recognition for it. Such feelings simply need to be given more recognition, appreciation, and prominence in our education and media, above the more animal satisfactions of food, clothing, and possessions.

From a Buddhist bioethical perspective, peace with nature and peace with humankind are inescapably connected to peace within the human being. But the recent and rapid industrialization and urbanization of Asia has had even more disastrous effects on the peace of mind of Asia's traditional societies than it had on those of Europe a century ago.

I have taught philosophy in Japan to over a thousand students in the past ten years. On the whole they are bright, hard-working, well-intentioned people. But they feel a deep sense of uncertainty, of instability, of rootlessness; they are seeking with little satisfaction for some sense and meaning in their hectic lives. The same is true of their parents' generation. The stresses, the tensions, the lack of clear values and meaning in the lives of the working generation of businessmen in urban Japan is approaching crisis proportions. It leads to futile attempts to find meaning or forget meaninglessness through sex, liquor, or overwork. The centuries-old extended family is forgotten as the urban worker moves from one tiny flat to another, detached from friends, relations, and traditions.

While yesterday's diseases were born from germs and bacteria, today's killer diseases are plainly the result of an overstressed, under-loved life style, and from carcinogenic attempts to escape it. Even when patients are hospitalized, they find not peace, but sterile and impersonal bureaucracies of masked biologists, each with their own special function. Few caregivers have time to be concerned with the spiritual crisis of life style, the lack of peace which precipitated the stroke, heart attack, or cancer in the first place. Even those most crucial of rites of passage: birth, marriage, and death, have been secularized and industrialized to the extent that celebration and grief are all condensed into prescribed hours and days, rather than becoming a process of spiritual purification and discovery. How can modern persons find peace in their spiritual and emotional lives amid a society which seems to place emphasis only on time and money?

Naturally, Buddhists have a crucial role to play in this arena of human peace—indeed, if Buddhism does not address the peace of the human being, it is doubtful that any other institution can do so either. Buddhist institutions and ceremonies have given people a sense of their belonging to a community. Such feelings of belonging are more important than ever today. Some urban temples in Japan have in fact instituted new festivals, ancestor-honoring days, and community purification days, which have resulted in improved human relations, lower crime rates, and a greater sense of peace and well-being of their communities.

In most traditional Asian societies, it was the grandparents who cared for the children while the young to middle-aged parents worked in the fields or local manufacturing. With the breakdown of the extended family and growth of nuclear couples, both the retired elderly and the youth find themselves under-cared-for and under-loved. Urbanization may make it impossible for all grandparents to live with their own grandchildren. But it is quite possible for every grandparent to live with *some* grandchildren, and indeed some very successful senior citizen/nursery schools have followed precisely this principle. The elders can teach and discipline the children, while passing on the wisdom of many years' experience. At the same time, the presence of children gives the elders interest, inspiration, a reason for living and wanting to see another day. Buddhists in Japan are beginning to establish *viharas* in which such intergenerational interdependence is healthfully reinforced while parents are busy at their respective jobs.

Whether Christian, Buddhist, or Confucian, the religious traditions speak to the higher value of spiritual than of material riches, to the peace of spirit found through the pursuit of altruism rather than of self-centered goals. This message most profoundly needs communicating and proclaiming in an age which tends to view persons as things and value them only for their material wealth.

Oversimplified, if humans fail to find peace in their own beings, they will continue to harbor greed, jealousy, antagonism, superiority and inferiority complexes—and as long as these complexes rule their emotional and behavioral lives, peace on a regional or world scale is yet far off. Conversely speaking, it is the finding of one's own happiness in another's victory, finding one's own peace in participation with a family or community of like-minded people, which can establish the basis for peace on every level. This is precisely the spiritual state toward which Buddhists are striving, albeit in various forms and languages.

While individual Buddhist sects have set up hospitals, schools, and homes for the elderly, orphaned, and handicapped, there is much that remains to be done in this area. Particularly in the area of religious counseling within the hospital and welfare home setting, as long as religions are seen as separate doctrinal camps, their presence in public hospitals and care institutions will be suspect, if not prohibited, as is the case in Japan. However, if the leaders of many sects can band together to voice the importance of spiritual support in the caring professions, this appeal will be seen not as a single doctrinal proselytizing, but as a psychological fact, and hospitals and homes will become more receptive to the values of religious volunteerism, which are the underpinning of much hospice and home-care work in the West. Even in projects such as disaster relief, where Buddhist offers of assistance are unlikely to be rebuffed, coordination of efforts at the highest levels can improve timing and effectiveness and reduce duplication of effort among well-intentioned but overlapping Buddhist aid groups.

The Noble Path of Tolerance, Forgiveness, Humility, Equanimity

Until recently, violence against nature was considered to be less pressing a problem than violence between humans. Traditional discussions of peace naturally concerned themselves with the elimination of war, strife, social violence, and crime. Improvements in medicine allowed populations to rise beyond the limits of local food supplies. The threats to peace are legion and hardly require a catalogue, but for the sake of specificity, let us recall just a few. Among the most glaring are the standoff between the two Koreas, a relic of long and bitter hot and cold wars; the continuing strife in Indochina, with its consequent refugee problems in Laos and Thailand; the internal revolutions in Buddhist Myanmar and Sri Lanka; the continuing religious struggles in India, the Middle East, Ireland, and the Balkans. This ethnic and regional violence is often repressed by the governments of the respective regions, leading in turn to the imprisonment and abuse of people thought dangerous to the regime; this has included many Buddhist priests in Southeast Asia. In addition, crime has reached epidemic proportions, not only in the drug-producing regions of the "golden triangle," but particularly in metropolises like Hong Kong, Manila, and Dhaka, followed by other capital cities growing out of control. What can Buddhists or enlightened ethical people of goodwill do to work for social peace here?

On the international and political front, Buddhists serve as a powerful force for peace. They can organize non-violent marches and protests against the violence of armed forces. They can offer the locations and personnel to serve as negotiators between parties in political conflict. Buddhists all have a mutual interest in maintaining the freedom to practice their own beliefs, and can pressure politicians to free political captives while pressuring political outsiders to avoid recourse to violence. They can establish camps for refugees and programs for their assimilation into a new society.

But peace will remain a futile dream as long as major segments of the populations are malnourished, homeless, sick, and oppressed. A prerequisite for social peace and the elimination of criminal violence is the guarantee of certain minimal levels of livelihood and well-being. Here too, religious organizations can play a major role. In some cities, religions have set up halfway houses for the rehabilitation of homeless prostitutes and drug addicts, so that they might return to leading constructive human lives. In other communities, temples have set up standing committees for relief of disaster areas. Whenever a flood, fire, volcano, or epidemic breaks out, teams of members are immediately ready to lend food, materials, and manpower toward the restoration of peace and stability in the disaster area. Throughout history, Buddhists have worked subtly but significantly for peace by advocating a redistribution of wealth—by accepting donations from the rich and conveying them to the poor who most need the basic necessities of life. Not as a doctrine or sect, but as a philosophical perspective on life, Buddhism can contribute toward peace and social security on local, regional, and international levels.

The idea that humans can be enemies is our biggest enemy. We face a big job in the re-education of our citizenries. One hundred years ago, most of the countries of Asia did not exist as countries; their present boundaries were imposed only by colonial imperialism and the standoff of internal warfare. Ironically, it was often religion which encouraged the belief in the "rightness" and superiority of each community's convictions, and hence led to intolerance of other religions and ethnicities. The time has come when the small gods of region, language, and ethnicity need to be set aside for the larger truth of a world family. Religions need not relinquish their claims to spiritual insight, but they can admit the value of other religions, and above all teach tolerance, cooperation, and non-violence in the reform of situations in need of change.

On a personal level, real peace will not be achieved until expression of hate, bigotry, and greed have been overcome. This is a tall order, but precisely what Buddhism asks of us: the virtues of friendliness, compassion, peace of mind, equanimity. In this sense, a more Buddhist consciousness is ultimately prerequisite to the elimination of violence.

PRACTICAL ETHICAL EDUCATION

From Values Clarification to Values Communication

Early attempts to teach ethics in school classrooms were often predicated on religious values. This is not surprising, since religions have from ancient times expressed great concern in the matters of morals and ethics. However, whether the teaching were Shinto, Christian, or Buddhist, explicitly religious teaching became unacceptable because it necessarily left out or discriminated against those who did not share those same religious beliefs. As the separation of church and state has become increasingly thorough, the undesirability of teaching religion in the public schools has sometimes even been used as a reason not to teach ethics or morality at all.

One attempt to escape the charge of religious sectarianism was an American curriculum called "values clarification," developed in the 1970s. In this curriculum, students were presented with moral problems, dilemmas, and choices, and encouraged to express their own preferences about what should be done in each case. Rather than judging "better" and "worse" responses, the teacher served as a "facilitator" to try to get all of the students to express their visceral opinions and see what everyone thought.

Values clarification failed miserably to teach values of any kind. For one thing, expressing preferences is not the same as moral reasoning. Most students' values were illogical if not inchoate, sometimes self-contradictory or incoherent, almost always inadequately reasoned. In the absence of any instruction in how to reason morally, students' discussions ended in mere expression of personal preferences. Indeed, this often had the counterproductive result of giving students the false impression that moral choices are nothing more than personal preferences, and that there are no more definite grounds for moral decision-making. This was just the opposite result of what was originally desired.

When all of the opinions of all of the students were expressed and discussed, the conclusion was always something like, "So that's what we think! Aren't there a lot of different ways of looking at this issue!" and never a guidance toward a higher sense of morality. Governed by the prohibition against criticizing any particular student's views, the teachers were also prevented from taking a role of mentor, sage, or moral advisor. Many students wanted to look to their teachers as authority figures, especially on the issues of right and wrong. They lost confidence in their teachers, as well as in the very existence of right and wrong, when the teachers refused to take a stand and returned the problem to the students. So the "values clarification" technique failed to produce either moral reasoning, moral knowledge, or moral behavior.

However, there are programs of character education which inculcate morality of a non-sectarian sort, without prejudice against any religious or ethnic group. In these days of racial tensions, America is particularly sensitive to the dangers of religious or ethnic bias in its classrooms. Yet several highly successful programs of character curriculum have been developed which have offended none of the participants, and have produced very significant results for their schools.

One example is that of the American Institute for Character Education (AICE). The AICE Character Education Curriculum was developed in the 1970s and implemented in more than 45,000 classrooms in the 1980s. The AICE curriculum teaches such values as:

- Refusing narcotic drugs and alcohol

- Developing self-esteem, pride in school and community

- Respecting positive values and regarding the rights of others

- Setting goals and working toward them with self-discipline

- Taking responsibility for one's own behavior, resisting peer pressure

- Developing decision-making and problem-solving skills

- Cooperating with others, resolving conflicts

- Being on time and using time and talents efficiently

- Obeying rules and laws, respecting parents and teachers

- Honesty, equality, freedom, and justice

The AICE curriculum is scientifically designed to teach these values, without mentioning God or religion. It has been very successful. Many schools which have implemented this program have reported dramatic improvements in student behavior in the classroom and playground, decreased dropouts and increased school attendance. Ninety-three percent of teachers found improved self-concepts in students with low self-images, and 87 percent found improvements in students' spoken language.

In the beginning, schools feared that the time and money required to teach the new curriculum would be a problem. In fact, most teachers have found that after teaching character education, they have more time to teach other subjects, because the students are more attentive and well behaved. Schools found that the cost of materials and teacher training was more than offset by the savings in time spent in administrative disciplining of students and savings in the money spent on replacing school property broken or mistreated by students. So the program has proven time- and cost-effective.

Of course, each country and culture will have its own specific needs and its own most effective ways of teaching. While all of the values in the AICE curriculum are compatible with Buddhism, Japan might develop an even more Buddhist set, including ideas like the appreciation of beauty, caring for the living environment, and friendliness or compassion with other students. The important point to be noted here is that values can be taught effectively without dependence on particular sectarian religious creeds.

From Unintegrated Units to Education across the Curriculum

Japan's *Mombusho* (Ministry of Education) has already recognized the need for improved values education in the public schools, and it has already mandated the inclusion of new values teaching within the Social Studies Curriculum. However, the time set aside for such teaching is usually less than an hour a week. The teachers already feel overburdened with too much material to convey to the students in too little time. Few teachers have professional experience in teaching ethics and values, and there are few texts or teaching materials yet available.

While they do not fall into the trap of participatory values clarification, the texts used in teaching ethics in Japan are often historical accounts of the development of moral thinking, from Confucius and Aristotle through Marx and Mill. This historical survey approach has a double disadvantage. First, like the values clarification discussed above, it leaves the students with the relativistic idea that there are many possible views of ethics, but none demonstrably correct. Thus, it destroys rather than improves the students' ethical convictions. Second, by focusing on the abstract discussions of past ages, it reinforces the impression that ethics is a subject of long ago and far away, not something of immediate bearing on daily life. Such historical approaches remain on the desktop, and fail to affect the behavior of either students or teachers. Above all, the impact of one hour a week on the students is just too small to measure. So the present Japanese approach of adding one more unit to an already busy curriculum has been notably unsuccessful in changing the moral behaviors of the students.

However, there is a more effective approach, often called "across the curriculum" education. In this approach, the new material is not simply inserted in a separate period, but is rather integrated throughout many units of the existing curriculum. Some American junior high schools have used the AICE curriculum in this way, including it within lessons on language, social studies, arts, health, even biology. A more notable success is that of Marquette University in Wisconsin. Marquette recruited dozens of teachers to integrate an ethical component into their instruction in introductory courses ranging from nursing and dentistry to psychology, sociology, and literature. While relatively difficult across disciplinarily differentiated college courses, this approach should be even easier across junior and senior high school curricula.

Response of students and teachers to Marquette's "Ethics Across the Curriculum" approach (Ashmore and Starr 1991) has been unequivocally positive. They all learned that values and ethics are not a separate compartment of human life which a few people contemplate and most do not. Rather, ethics affects all aspects of our lives as social beings, and there are moral decisions to be made at every turn. Millennia ago, the Greeks considered literature and theater to be the stage for learning lessons of life. History can be a vehicle, not only for memorizing of names and dates, but for evaluating the effects of cruel or noble decisions on the people who experienced them. The sciences and professions have moral components in the ways that their knowledge is put to use, the ways their professionals relate to others, and the ways they demonstrate responsibility or irresponsibility to social and environmental issues. In short, effective ethics education is not compartmentalized into a specific time frame; rather, it is integrated throughout the system and across the curriculum.

From Lip-Service to Entrance Examinations and Hiring Practices

Even if character education is taught in every school, the grades which students achieve in their ethics classes have no effect on their futures. Ironically, the better the students, the more they disparage the present ethics curriculum. Many of my own former students now teach social studies in high schools around Japan. They report that in ethics classes, their best students take out math or English texts and ignore the ethics lessons. When the teachers demand that the students open their ethics texts, the unusually blunt response of many students is to ask the teacher, "Will this be on a college entrance exam? If not, then I will study what *will* be on the exam!"

The students' challenge is not a vacuous one; they are very perceptive. They have limited time, and they want to spend their time doing and learning that for which they will be ultimately rewarded. For a character education program to be effective, entrance exams to both colleges and corporations must include moral components. This is not difficult to do.

Colleges and employers can ask for letters of reference from the students' teachers, coaches, boy scout troop leaders, or bosses of part-time jobs, documenting specifically how the students do or do not demonstrate responsibility and morality. Psychological tests can show, with a high level of accuracy, how students will react to a wide variety of situations, and how strongly they are committed to certain moral positions. Such tests are already used in many sensitive high-security jobs, and by the government and military. Situational testing in the entrance or job-screening process can force applicants to choose between unethical practices with apparent personal benefits and ethical practices with greater expense or minor personal disadvantage.

Such testing does not infringe the rights of the applicants; rather it informs the applicants of the standards of the university or corporation to which they are applying before they enter it. Only when important corporations show that they are more interested in reliable, responsible, ethical workers than in workers with slightly higher math scores will students spend time thinking about how to be reliable and responsible rather than answering math problems.

From Unsupported Classrooms to Media Ideals

The Greeks knew that theater, more than being mere entertainment, had a powerful ethical influence on its spectators. Countless studies in recent years have demonstrated that cinema and television have far greater impact on the behaviors of their viewers than does comparable time spent in classrooms. Criminals have frequently testified that they gained from television both their desires to try some crime and their ideas of how to accomplish it. No matter how much time classroom teachers spend on ethical education, the impact of classroom teaching will remain low as long as their students spend even more time watching even more dramatic influences on television.

It would seem that the cinema and television industries have a vested interest in continuing to display sex, brutality, bad language, and immorality, for the more shocking the scenes, the more potential viewers may be attracted. As long as the media have such motivations, the spiral of immorality on the screen producing immorality in life will continue. This vicious circle needs to be cut at three different places, by three different groups: by the government, by the viewers, and by the industry itself.

In the face of massive evidence that media brutality produces real-life criminal behavior, there is no moral reason for government to refrain from censorship for the good of the people. Every government in every country practices some forms of censorship, restricting the parts of the body that can be depicted, and restricting direct appeals to overthrow the government by force. While there can be some debate about whether depicting the private parts encourages sexual immorality, there can no longer be debate about the fact that repeated depiction of criminal violence and brutality numbs the viewers to such violence, and in fact, glorifies such violence in the eyes of young viewers (cf. Yamanaka et al. 1986). If criminal violence is against the best interest of the community or state, then it is indeed the moral prerogative of the state or community to restrict the display of such violence.

Many families will agree to self-restrict their viewing if the moral contents of programs are made explicit before the programs are aired. In many communities of America and Britain, for example, television magazines clearly detail in advance which programs have nudity, sex, brutality, horror, strong or obscene language, and so on. On this basis, many parents restrict their children's viewing, and even limit their own. As producers find that their rating percentages are sometimes hurt rather than improved by sex and criminal violence, they will invest less time and money in this area, and more in shows which attract broader audiences.

From a more Buddhist perspective, it is indeed the responsibility of the industry to restrict itself to producing scenes and ideas of health and edification to the people. If even one station can take pride in producing programs which regularly glorify morality and elevate the consciousness of its viewers, it can gradually gain a reputation which others will want to emulate. To encourage this trend, foundations and non-governmental organizations can give prestige and/or financial awards to media which produce programs which glorify peaceful, virtuous, moral behavior, rather than highlighting violence or brutality. Just as stations now compete to produce the best singer, the best comedy, or the best special effects, they should be rewarded and encouraged to compete for prizes in the best character education and consciousness-lifting programs.

Making Morality Fashionable—Making Money from Morality

The change of society from self-aggrandizing to beauty-appreciating, from consumerist to conservationist, from valuing physical possessions to valuing natural experience, will not come quickly. But it must come, for if it does not, all of human society will perish in the cycle of consumption and pollution. At least in the transition—and perhaps in the long run—it will be necessary that people have monetary incentives to behave in new ways. When farmers find, for example, that they can sell more rice by growing it organically than with chemical fertilizers, more and more farmers will move to do so. When manufacturers find that their consumers want biodegradable detergents and recyclable paper, they will produce biodegradable detergents and recyclable paper.

Naturally, such changes depend on the raising of the consciousness of the average consumer. The consumer needs to realize that each time he or she makes a purchase, he or she is at the same time making a vote for the preservation of the industry producing that good or service, at the expense of all its competitors. In Buddhist terms, no action is an isolated event, but all is causally interdependent, and the *karmas* (actions) sown today will continue to have effects with reverberate down through the centuries. A growing realization of the causal interdependence of all beings is a minimal prerequisite to the ethical coming of age of our society.

CONCLUDING REMARKS

I have become known in Japan and abroad for my work in the study of Near-Death Experiences. Some people on the brink of death, or thought to be dead temporarily, recover long enough to report having had "Life Reviews" in which their whole lives passed before them, and they were forced to judge their lives themselves. Such people invariably report that more than all the money, fame, or glory achieved in the eyes of the world, their most positive moments were those when they had genuinely loved and assisted other living beings—and their most negative moments were those where they had harbored anger, hate, greed, or cravings. Many terminal patients who do not have full-fledged Near-Death Experiences also report similar realizations. While lying in their hospital beds and realizing that their days are now numbered, their minds inevitably return to review the events, large and small, of their former lives. The vast majority come to the humbling realization that the moments of which they can be proudest are precisely the moments when the (Buddhist) virtues of friendliness, compassion, joy, and equanimity were best expressed; and the moments they regret the most are those when they fell into animal desires or used other people as means to their own self-satisfactions. Such accounts give a valuable corrective perspective to our society's present overweening concerns with fame and money.

We have seen that an Eastern worldview well expressed by the fundamental tenets of Buddhism is eminently applicable to the problems of the contemporary world. We have proposed some ways that these worldviews and life styles can be communicated through schools, media, and business practices. The imbalances which humans have imposed on the ecosystem leave no choice as to whether or not these environmental ethics should be adopted. The only question is how soon they can be understood and practiced, and how many beings will suffer before that stage is reached.

REFERENCES

American Institute for Character Education pamphlets. San Antonio, Texas.
Ashmore, Robert B., and William C. Starr, eds. 1991. *Ethics Across the Curriculum: The Marquette Experience*. Milwaukee, WI: Marquette University Press.
Conze, Edward. 1959. *Buddhism: Its Essence and Development*. New York: Harper Torchbooks.
deBary, Wm. Theodore, ed. 1972. *The Buddhist Tradition in India, China, and Japan*. New York: Random House/Vintage Books.
Ishihara, John S. 1987. "A Shin Buddhist Social Ethics," *The Pure Land*, n.s. IV, December.
Jacobson, Nolan Pliny. 1983. *Buddhism and the Contemporary World: Change and Self-Correction*. Carbondale: Southern Illinois University Press.
Yamanaka, Hayato et al., eds. 1986. *Japanese Communication Studies of the 1970's*. Honolulu, HI: The East-West Center.

For Further Reading

Bowie, Norman E., and R. Edward Freeman, eds. 1992. *Ethics and Agency Theory.* New York: Oxford University Press.

Byrne, Peter. 1992. *Philosophical and Theological Foundations of Ethics.* London: Macmillan.

Carr, Brian, ed. 1996. *Morals and Society in Asian Philosophy.* Richmond, Surrey: Curzon.

Deigh, John, ed. 1992. *Ethics and Personality.* Chicago: University of Chicago Press.

Field, G. C. 1966. *Moral Theory: An Introduction to Ethics.* London: Methuen.

Fromm, Erich. 1949 and 1990. *Man for Himself: An Enquiry into the Psychology of Ethics.* London: Routledge and Kegan Paul.

Fu, C. W-H., and Sandra Wawrytko, eds. 1991. *Buddhist Ethics and Modern Society.* Westport, CT: Greenwood Press.

Hollingworth, Harry L. 1949. *Psychology and Ethics: A Study of the Sense of Obligation.* New York: Ronald Press.

Kalupahana, David. 1995. *Ethics in Early Buddhism.* Honolulu: University of Hawaii Press.

Keown, Damien. 1992. *The Nature of Buddhist Ethics.* London: Macmillan.

Keown, Damien. 1995. *Buddhism and Bioethics.* New York: St. Martin's Press.

Lacan, Jacques. 1992. *Ethics of Psychoanalysis.* Dennis Porter, trans. New York: Norton.

Levine, Maurice. 1972. *Psychiatry and Ethics.* New York: G. Braziller.

McGrath, Elizabeth Z. 1994. *The Art of Ethics: A Psychology of Ethical Beliefs.* Chicago: Loyola University Press.

Nakasone, Ronald Y. 1990. *Ethics of Enlightenment: In Search of a Buddhist Ethic.* San Francisco: Dharma Cloud.

Prebish, Charles. 1992. *Buddhist Ethics: A Cross-Cultural Approach.* Dubuque, IA: Kendall Hunt.

Saddhatissa, Hammalawa. 1970. *Buddhist Ethics: The Essence of Buddhism*. London: Allen and Unwin.

Schlick, Moritz, Josef Schachter, and Friedrich Waismann. 1994. *Ethics and the Will*. Hans Kaal, trans. (Vienna Circle Collection). New York: Kluwer Academic.

Steere, Jane. 1984. *Ethics in Clinical Psychology*. New York: Oxford University Press.

Swearer, Donald, and R. F. Sizemore, eds. 1990. *Ethics, Wealth, and Salvation: A Study in Buddhist Social Ethics*. Charleston: University of South Carolina Press.

Szasz, Thomas. 1988. *The Ethics of Psychoanalysis: Theory and Method of Autonomous Psychotherapy*. Syracuse, NY: Syracuse University Press.

Tachibana, S. 1992. *The Ethics of Buddhism*. Richmond, Surrey: Curzon.

Tiwary, Mahesh, ed. 1989. *Perspectives on Buddhist Ethics*. New Delhi: Delhi University.

Urmson, J. O. 1968. *The Emotive Theory of Ethics*. London: Hutchinson.

Wallwork, Ernest. 1991. *Psychoanalysis and Ethics*. New Haven, CT: Yale University Press.

Wunderlich, Dale P. 1985. *Towards a Foundation for Ethics in Education Administration*. Ann Arbor, MI: UMI.

Index

About the Editor and Contributors

ROBERT AZIZ is a psychotherapist in private practice in London, Ontario. He is a clinical member of the Ontario Society of Psychotherapists, and a part-time lecturer at the University of Western Ontario Faculty of Continuing Education. He is the author of *C. G. Jung's Psychology of Religion and Synchronicity* (1990), and is writing a second book on the clinical implications of synchronicity.

CARL B. BECKER is Professor of Comparative Cultures at Kyoto University, and Affiliate Researcher at the International Research Center for Japanese Studies. He is a Director of the Japan Holistic Medical Association, the Biothanatology Association, the International Society for Life Information Science, and an editor of the journal *Mortality*. His books include *American and English Ideals* (1991), *At the Border of Death* (1992), *Breaking the Circle: Buddhist Views of Death and Afterlife* (1993), and *After All: Issues of Life and Death* (1998).

ROBERT BOSNAK is a Jungian psychoanalyst, and graduated from the C. G. Jung Institute in Zurich in 1977. He is a member of the International Association for Analytical Psychology, the National Association for the Advancement of Psychoanalysis, and the Japanese Association for Clinical Psychology. His *Little Course in Dreams* (1988) is published in twelve languages, including Japanese; more recently, he has authored *Tracks in the Wilderness of Dreaming* (1997).

STEPHEN KARCHER is a writer, lecturer, and personal consultant who has worked with and repeatedly translated the *I Ching, the Classic of*

Change. Past Director of Research at the Eranos Foundation, he holds doctorates in comparative literature and archetypal psychology. His latest books are *The Illustrated Encyclopedia of Divination* (1997) and *How to Use the I Ching* (1998); his *Ta Chuan: The Great Treatise*, a new translation of a classical Chinese text on divination, spirituality, and ethical behavior, is soon to be released.

DAVID R. LOY is a Professor in the Faculty of International Studies at Bunkyo University, Chigasaki, Japan. His work primarily compares Buddhist with modern Western thought. In addition to scholarly papers in professional journals, he has authored *Nonduality: A Study in Comparative Philosophy* (1989) and *Lack and Transcendence: The Problem of Death and Life in Psychotherapy, Existentialism, and Buddhism* (1996).